POETRY MATTERS

Edited by Helen Davies

Poems From The Midlands

First published in Great Britain in 2011 by:

 Young**Writers**

Remus House
Coltsfoot Drive
Peterborough
PE2 9BF
Telephone: 01733 890066
Website: www.youngwriters.co.uk

Foreword

Since our inception in 1991, Young Writers has endeavoured to promote poetry and creative writing within schools by running annual nationwide competitions. These competitions are designed to develop and nurture the burgeoning creativity of the next generation, and give them valuable confidence in their own abilities.

This regional anthology is one of the series produced by our latest secondary school competition, *Poetry Matters*. Using poetry as their tool, the young writers were given the opportunity to tell the world what matters to them. The authors of our favourite three poems were also given the chance to appear on the front cover of their region's collection.

Whilst skilfully conveying their opinions through poetry, the writers showcased in this collection have simultaneously managed to give poetry a breath of fresh air, brought it to life and made it relevant to them. Using a variety of themes and styles, our featured poets leave a lasting impression of their inner thoughts and feelings, making this anthology a rare insight into the next generation.

Contents

The Poems

Discovery Cove

Hip, hip hooray!
Today's my birthday!
I made my bed, went and got fed,
Then thought about the day ahead.

Luckily the car journey was short and sweet,
Because it was hard to cope in the boiling heat.
At Discovery Cove there was a huge queue,
But within 15 minutes we were through.

I struggled with my wetsuit, raring to go,
With excitement whizzing from my head to my toe.
I eventually reached the soft, yellow sand,
And amazing experience in the palm of my hand.

The day promised adventure and fun,
With a sky so blue and the warmth from the sun.
The lagoons were full of tropical fish
And wait for it, it gets better than this.

Swam with stingrays, all smooth and sweet
And came face to face with barracuda teeth.
Relaxed in a luxurious, lukewarm lagoon,
Getting even more excited as the dolphins were coming soon.

When the time to swim with the dolphins finally arrived,
I looked around to see gleaming eyes.
We dipped out feet into the freezing cold pool,
Then found out Akai was what our dolphin was called.

We each had a go and got a salty, wet kiss
And fed Akai a frozen, smelly fish.
We had a speedy ride on his fin
And stroked his scratched and rubbery skin.

But it came the time when we had to say goodbye,
And not surprisingly everyone gave a great big sigh.
I took one more look at the magnificent scene
And thought, what a wonderful birthday this has been!

Harry Dovey (12)
Abington High School, Wigston

Just The Everyday Things

I see the sun shining bright on a summer's day,
The children outside, ready to play.
The trees swaying in the summer breeze,
I hear the sound of an old man's sneeze.
I see the wildly overgrown grass,
As I watch the school kids heading to class.
I hear the bell ring like a charm,
I see the cattle in the barn.
I watch the sky go from bright to dark,
I hear a dog loudly bark,
I sit and listen to the wind whistle,
It's very sharp, like a thistle.

The sun's rising for a new day
And once again the kids are out to play.
Summer's almost over and the cold weather's here,
It's nearly time for a brand new year.
I see the sales for the Christmas shop,
I hear the rain begin to drop.
I watch the kids have their last day at school,
They think it's actually really cool.
I see people giving presents and cards,
We all have the snow-covered yards.
I hear the sounds of people's joy,
As I see the kids with their new toy.

Now it's nearly the New Year,
When people start to cheer.
The TV's on and the countdown starts,
'3, 2, 1, Happy New Year,' comes out like a dart.
Now we all have to wait,
For the exact same date.

Chloe Harper (13)
Abington High School, Wigston

The Cricket Match

Leicestershire to bat, they win the toss,
We are happy, they are cross,
But out they come, ready to battle,
The crowd clap, cheer and tittle tattle.

The teams are ready, the bowler to send
That first ball from the pavilion end.
He runs up at medium pace,
The batsman hits and the fielders chase.

160-6, the batsman doesn't delay,
Only five more overs left to play.
The ball is bowled, it's just like a missile,
Clean takes, middle stump, the crowd start to whistle.

190-7, after Leicestershire's innings,
15,000 supporters all clapping and singing.
Hampshire's turn to bat, bat for their life,
Hoping that bad light doesn't stop play at 20 to 5.

The batsmen are ready, the bowler poised,
All the time trying to block out the noise.
The ball is hit long, the fielders run around,
But only to dismay, the ball is caught high in the crowd.

It's all square with five overs to play,
Overhead it's looking grey.
Both teams rush through the overs,
The groundsmen all ready to bring out the covers.

The final over, 9 to win,
The bowler runs up, let the over begin.
Two more runs and it's a draw . . .
The greatest game I ever saw.

James Garratt (13)
Abington High School, Wigston

I See The Sky

A shatter of light, piercing,
Piercing through the darkness.
A dance of glitter giving life
To the blank, vast canvas of space.

The cool, refreshing breeze tickles my body,
Swirling around my face and arms.
I am staring like an idiot or a fool would,
Or perhaps as a child may, gazing on the stars.

I look far above me, stretching my view,
Stretching it to where I can imagine
Imagine a thousand stars, surrounded,
Surrounded by a million planets.

It is quiet, not a deathly quiet,
Awkward quiet or suspicious quiet,
Just peacefully quiet as I stare upon the sky.
The deep black, yet blue and yet lighter blue upon the blueness
Breaking up the dark, soulless place.

It may be my mind or the truth
But I see the sky and I see beyond,
I see the authentic and exotic swirls of colour,
Colour spreading into the stars and exploding with amazement.

I should put this down to a dream,
If only I were asleep.
But the thing about dreams, even about the night
You don't want to wake up.

Harry Jackson (13)
Abington High School, Wigston

I Am Slave

The whipping and hurting,
The names and abuse,
It's the price I pay,
Staying in recluse.

Being sent overseas,
Or dragged to the rich,
Seeing my family kidnapped,
Being accused as a witch.

The shouting and screaming,
The trade and the money,
I hate it all,
It's not funny.

A slave's work is hard,
With no pay and no choice,
My thoughts are destroyed,
I have no voice.

I want to escape,
Get out of this world,
Stop the whipping and the hitting
And bodies being hurled.

Despite the rules and hurt,
I've nowhere else to go,
Slavery is all I've got,
It's very sad, I know.

Rebecca Cawthorn (14)
Abington High School, Wigston

The Creature Of The Forest

In a realm of magic, far away,
Full of lies and deception,
There be a child, lost in the forest, a stray,
Never to be found again . . .

As she wanders, lost and alone,
With no sense of direction,
The eerie silence send chills to her bones,
Feeling nothing but fear and pain.

She finds dead bodies scattered across the floor,
As she begins to tremble in fright.
She turns around, only to find more,
Through fear she runs as fast as she can.

Trying to escape the fate of those men,
An evil creature of the night,
But all is lost as she falls into the fen,
A poor girl, never to reach womanhood.

She hears something coming,
Running through the woods,
There's an evil demon, her death he is scheming,
How much longer does she have?

She whispers her last prayers,
Takes her last breath.
Here it comes, her slayer,
As she invites in Death.

Talia Holmes (12)
Abington High School, Wigston

Just Think

Put it down,
You don't have to carry that around,
Put it down, just put it down.

Just think about the lives,
Don't draw for the gun or the knife,
What's great about stabbing a man and seeing him wail?
Because you'll probably end up in jail.

Road idols, street titles,
Gun on, gun gang rivals,
Honestly, what are we achieving?
Is killing really what you believe in?

When you pull the knife out of your pocket,
Think to yourself, *Stop it!*
When you have your finger on the trigger
Just think, *This gun isn't a winner.*

Knife and gun crime isn't good,
It only sheds tears and blood,
So don't carry guns or knives,
Because you'll be wasting people's lives.

Put it down,
You don't have to carry that around,
Put it down, just put it down.

Christopher Wardley (13)
Abington High School, Wigston

Moving Out

Today's the day we're moving out,
So excited, but still in doubt,
We've packed our bags and ready to go,

Hopefully it doesn't snow,
In the van, we're on our way,
So excited, it's our first day!

Megan Edwards (12)
Abington High School, Wigston

Christmas

I can hear the carols being sung by children,
I can see the sale signs in the shops,
I can taste the mince pies on my tongue,
It can only mean one thing;
Christmas is here.

Mum and Dad are defrosting the turkey,
Me and my sister are decorating the tree,
We're wrapping presents for friends and family,
This can only mean one thing;
It's Christmas Eve.

No one can sleep that night,
The minutes seem like hours
And the hours seem like days,
This can only mean one thing;
It's Christmas tomorrow!

The family is arriving,
The presents are open,
Christmas is special,
But this can only mean one thing;
Christmas is nearly over!

Chloe Jones (13)
Abington High School, Wigston

The Sherlock Holmes Limerick

A great detective was Sherlock,
He could see who had broken the lock,
A woman was dead
With a bruise on her head,
He deduced it in the tick of a clock!

Iziah Murphy-Lee (13)
Abington High School, Wigston

Come On Leicester

Just one season ago
Leicester were the best,
Heading for promotion,
Better than the rest.

But, oh no, disaster struck!
A new manager we had,
Unfortunately this time
He was very, very bad!

From the beginning
He had no respect.
Everyone doubted
If he could finish our quest.

We are currently bottom,
The blame lies with him.
Will he get going
Because our future looks grim?

But now things look good,
Another boss is here,
He's Sven Goran Eriksson,
Premier League this time next year!

Liam Sandhu (11)
Abington High School, Wigston

My Fish, Patch

My fish, Patch, is white and gold,
He swims really slowly because he's so old.
When I come down in the morning he's staring at me,
I say, 'Hey Patch, cup of tea?'
His mouth opens and closes as if to say,
'Good morning, how are you? Have a good day.'
My fish, Patch, he's so cool,
I wish one day I could take him to school.

Thomas Ward (11)
Abington High School, Wigston

My Little Dog
(Something important to me)

Tilly is my special dog,
She eats and eats just like a hog.
Spends her day on the armchair,
She's covered with many brown hairs.

I take her to the park with her ring and ball,
She runs and runs till she takes a fall.
The one thing she hates the most,
Is when my mum feeds her toast.

She can jump through hoops,
Run around in loops,
Give me a high five,
Set the house alive,
Hop up high,
Make my mum sigh,
Bark really loud,
This is why I'm so proud.

Emily Martin (12)
Abington High School, Wigston

The Bullet With No Name

Children playing in the park,
Laugh and joke as they are watched,
Here I sit and watch them play,
Remembering the day a life was taken away.
Bullets were flying everywhere,
Children were crying out in fear,
Parents searching everywhere,
But as I look towards the ground,
I can still see that poor child laying down,
For that life was taken away,
By the bullet which did carry no name.

Joseph Parry (14)
Abington High School, Wigston

Tiger Trauma

Sleek, fast, nimble and mean,
The tiger really is a killing machine,
But the tiger's in trouble,
Hunted to extreme.
Poachers kill for meat, for fur and bone,
The shots they fire make a deafening tone,
They think the tiger is magic,
The story behind is quite tragic.
No potion or lotion will work on these foes,
Yet they have caused the tiger many woes.
Soon there will be no tigers left on this planet,
This cannot be right, can it?

Christopher Holdridge (11)
Abington High School, Wigston

X Factor

Every weekend
Between seven and eight,
I watch X Factor
Because I think it's great!

Louis is old!
Cheryl is thin!
Danni is an Aussie and
Simon just wants to win!

The boys, girls, groups and others
Sing to stay in the show,
The public have to choose their favourite,
But one has to go.

It comes to the final week,
When they announce who's won,
The winner releases a song
To make a Christmas number one!

Isla Crane (11)
Abington High School, Wigston

Food

Food can be tiny or fill up your plate,
When there is food on the table I won't be late.
There are all different sizes, brands and makes,
Like pizza, gammon and big, yummy cakes.
But one appetiser that I really like,
It's not any fish like cod or pike,
But it's bread, it's weird, I know
And I love it when it's war, all the fresh dough.
I like original, tiger tail and seeded bread,
Every day I can't get it out of my head.
Now you know I love bread,
But what food do you like?

Benjamin Allardyce (11)
Abington High School, Wigston

Big Barry Gears

As Sir reads the list
There's only one name I hear
This one's my arch-nemesis
He's Big Barry Gears

As I hear that snigger
It's like I've pulled that trigger
He's left me in tears
That's Big Barry Gears

It's lunchtime now
I hear his howl
I've been hunted like deers
By Big Barry Gears

I'm battered and bruised
It's just old news
Only two more years
With that Big Barry Gears!

Jack Murphy (14)
Abington High School, Wigston

Why Me

Every day's the same,
Slap after slap,
It doesn't stop,
I wish it would end.

I feel small,
I can't do anything about it,
Someone, help me, now,
I'm a kid no one cares about.

I scream and shout,
But no one hears me out,
Sometimes I think to myself
Why am I living like this?

I can't live like this,
I wish I could go to sleep
And everything would be fine,
But not when you're me.

Jessica Hewitt (13)
Abington High School, Wigston

My Family

Family will always be there for you,
Family will always stay true.
My family are the best,
They're better than all the rest.
My sister is cool;
She works so hard at school.
My dad's in the force
And keeps me on course.
My mum's a nurse;
She carries the family purse.
I love my family.

Joe Chamberlain (11)
Abington High School, Wigston

Me And My Dog

Me and my dog,
He's my best friend,
We do everything together,
From the start to the end.

We go on adventures,
Big and small,
From the park to the beach,
We've done them all.

When I'm upset or feeling sick,
He snuggles up close
And gives me a lick!

Me and my dog,
He's my best friend,
We do everything together,
From start to the end.

Laura Heybrock (12)
Abington High School, Wigston

Save Our Pandas

We love pandas,
Yes we do,
Their homes are going
Because of you.

They don't deserve this,
So what can we do?
If we don't save them
They will just be in the zoo.

Poor, poor pandas,
Why should they die?
Please don't make
Them say goodbye.

Jennifer Witts (11)
Abington High School, Wigston

Little Big Planet

L ittle sack people
I n
T he
T iny
L ittle
E arth

B right colours
I magination overload
G reat sun

P S3
L ots of movement
A nimation
N ight-time adventure
E ntertainment
T ime to party.

Lauren Cox (11)
Abington High School, Wigston

Stand Up, Salute

Dig for oil!
Hunt for gold!
In the last few years
The Earth's problems have unfolded,
Litter, pollution and global warming,
This is the Earth's final warning!
So the more shall we recycle,
So less shall we pollute
And to the people that want to make this happen
Stand up, salute!

Jack Gabriel (13)
Abington High School, Wigston

A Special Place

Sometimes, when your heart grows weary,
And cope you cannot,
You just want to escape from reality.

You want to go to a place
Where problems are a thing of the past.
You want to go to a place
Where pain and sorrow are no more.

I have no place as such,
I am forced to wander on,
The weight of emotion holding me back.

For, I wish
People saw the fury behind my eyes,
I wish people saw me for me,
Not who I pretend to be.

Josette Punter-Thomas (12)
Abington High School, Wigston

The Jump Bike King

J ump bikes are really cool
U p in the air they fly
M ine is so colourful
P eople stop and stare when I'm in the air

B *ang!* As I crash back down
I njured, down on the floor
K ing is about to roar
E veryone gathers round
S o sorry people begin to sound.

Jack Harding (11)
Abington High School, Wigston

Brothers

We have a bond by blood
That ties us still
Through time if bad and good
Annoying habits irritate
But still we share a love
That evolves through care
Of each other's being
Never to be divided
Or undone
We stand proud and protective
Of each and everyone
Brothers by blood
Nothing can divide
Together, forever, we are tied.

Darien Pereira (13)
Abington High School, Wigston

The Fallen

The child wails for lack of food,
The mother rocks her gently to sleep,
To dream of battle and of death,
She tosses and turns in her crib and wakes
Into a living nightmare.

The soldier closes his eyes and dreams of peace and home,
He dreams of family and friends
And of a world without gunfire,
But wakes to the sound of death.

I walk towards the fallen,
With arms open in welcome,
To guide them to death,
Today I claim one more,
For I am the Angel of Death.

Heather Proudman (12)
Abington High School, Wigston

Winning The Game

Coming up to 90 minutes,
Everything was still even,
Running up and down the pitch,
Frantically, like lightning.
A player on the other team shot,
Just skimmed by the post,
Then, all of a sudden,
I felt the football at my feet.
No one was marking me,
I dribbled it closer to goal,
I shot and watched it fly through the air,
It hit the back of the net.
My team are running up to me,
I had won the game.

Lauren Jones (12)
Abington High School, Wigston

The Darkness

If only it were so simple,
To cruise through life smelling roses,
But obstacles blacken the countryside
And we unwittingly crush them beneath our feet.

Dreams sustain us, then the stress comes,
Goals give us the strength to finish,
Yet they change with every turn, around every obstacle
And remain unbeatable through out the time you have left.

Mistakes are made and regrets will be regretted,
You wish you had never done the thing you regret most,
The victories are flashes of light,
Sudden and not lasting,
Which allow us to glimpse the road ahead,
Before darkness.

Charlotte Bell (11)
Abington High School, Wigston

Poverty

Thousands die from poverty each year,
But thankfully we're all right here,
Most die from hunger and thirst,
But others die from cold and no care.

Poverty happens in poorer countries,
Where people get ill and don't get better.
Poverty makes most homeless and cold,
Whilst others sit careless at home,
People can't help it when they're ill,
Because the doctor's way over the hill.

In this country most live in peace,
But some still don't have enough to eat,
Poverty does kill millions a year,
When will poverty ever stop?

Hema Bowe (13)
Abington High School, Wigston

Holidays

H i, my name is Jai, I'm
O ut in the sun all day.
L ollipops to lick,
I ce creams to eat,
D rinks to sip
A ll day!
Y ou should come and join me,
S o grab your bucket and spade!

Jai Mistry (12)
Abington High School, Wigston

Memories

Memories are wonderful things
You cherish and love them so.
You may even become a king
But you'll never forget
That big show.

Sometimes they're bad
The ones that always stay.
The good memories you always had
They slowly fade away.

Elise Ford (11)
Abington High School, Wigston

Fashion

Leggings and jeggings,
Uggs and high heels,
Pink tops and black tops,
All the best deals.

Hair up in a pony,
Down, long and straight,
Curls round and bouncy,
Looking just great!

Melissa Moore (11)
Abington High School, Wigston

Nature - Haiku

A glittering lake,
The sweet smell of lavender,
A cloud of green leaves.

Sarah Cooper (12)
Brewood CE Middle School, Brewood

The Seaside

Look at me
Here I am, splashing in the sea
It has gorgeous views
But still I wear my wet shoes.

Look at me,
I've found a shell
It's my 9th, I'm doing well
In the sun my shells do shine
I'm so glad that they are mine.

Look at me
I'm building a castle of sand
It's the greatest in the land
I beat my mom, I beat my dad
Because theirs were really bad!

Look at me
It's the end of the day
We are at the shop
I have got a stick of rock
My mom got a golden clock.

Look at me, I'm all wet
But I've had the best day yet!

Ellena Green (11)
Brewood CE Middle School, Brewood

Dad

I brushed my teeth and combed my hair,
You used to drive me everywhere,
You'd hold my hand and never let go,
Oh how I hope my love did show
And when I needed you the most,
You were always there and did stay close,
Oh Dad, how I love you so.

You're my sunshine on a rainy day,
You're my shining star, you guide the way
And when you're gone even for one day
I miss you so when you're away,
The tears form in my eyes,
You're not here now when I cry.
Oh Dad, how I miss you so.

When you return through the front door,
I don't think I've loved you so much before,
My heart starts thumping hard,
I'll love you near or far,
Then you hug me and hold me tight,
I feel I might cry, I just might,
Right now there's a connection, a spark.
A spark in my heart.
Dad, I love you!

Emilee Hutchinson (12)
Brewood CE Middle School, Brewood

Old, Lonely Man

What do you see nurses?
What do you see?
What are you thinking when you're looking at me?
An old, elderly man, a man that can't hear,
When you want to be heard you have to come near.
As wrinkly as a raisin, with thin, white hair,
When you look at me you don't care.
You think we're impossible, but you don't really try,
You have to be patient, that makes me cry.
I am weak and feeble and I need extra support,
I'm not young, I don't do physical sport.
Is that what you're thinking?
Is that what you see?
Then open your eyes Nurse,
You're not looking at me.
I'm not who you think I am, I'm not dull.
A young boy of ten with a father and mother,
Two older sisters and a younger brother.
A teenager now and my dreams are clear,
Being a footballer, it's coming near.
Twenty-one and I'm happily married,
Our first babies are ready to be carried.
At forty now, my kids are growing fast,
Our family love will always last.
At fifty now and life is going quick,
My life is burning away, like a candle wick.
I'll soon have to face that dreaded day,
Sitting here now, with my young boy still inside,
My heart made of stone, pumping my mind.
In my life these emotions I've had,
I remember the good, I remember the bad.
So open your eyes Nurse, open and see,
I'm not a lonely old man, look closer, see me.

Will Twigger (12)
Brewood CE Middle School, Brewood

An Unkempt Half-Hearted Town

An unkempt, half-hearted town,
A damp, dark and deserted place,
The stench of rotten dustbins reaches your nose,
The sound of smashing windows and screeching cars
can be heard for miles around.

The sky is as black as coal;
The blurry mist hits your face
Sending a shiver down your spine,
You can see the sad, miserable paint has been carelessly thrown onto the
houses.

In the middle of nowhere,
A place of death,
No one to be seen,
Nothing.

How can we help towns like these?
We must cure them,
We must help them recover,
We will make them happy.

Joe Pugh (12)
Brewood CE Middle School, Brewood

My Nan

As sweet as sugar,
A brilliant hugger,
Always on my mind,
She's one of a kind!
She's calm and gentle,
Never judgmental,
She's warm-hearted and funny,
Makes my day sunny,
That's why I love her,
She's my grandmother!

Olivia Carmell (11)
Brewood CE Middle School, Brewood

Reverie

(An extract)

I linger by the bubbling stream,
My heart is glowing,
Lifting my self-esteem,
The world is whizzing past, growing.

All at once I see,
To my surprise
Daisies growing all around me,
The sound of birds in song rise.

I linger by the bubbling stream,
My heart is glowing,
Lifting my self-esteem,
The world is whizzing past, growing.

Suddenly, up in the sky
A row of colours arch,
They dance, way up high,
In the ground, reaching up, is a larch.

I linger by the bubbling stream,
My heart is glowing,
Lifting my self-esteem,
The world is whizzing past, growing.

Diving down is a flash of blue,
Entering like a dart,
His aim forever true,
A kingfisher's art.

I linger by the bubbling stream,
My heart is glowing,
Lifting my self-esteem,
The world is whizzing past, growing.

A low croaking sound,
The frog has seen a fly,
Leaping up from the ground,
To catch it he will try.

I linger by the bubbling stream,
My heart is glowing,

Lifting my self-esteem,
The world is whizzing past, growing.
Pink lilies in flower,
Brighten up the dullest day,
Their loveliness will never cower,
Different colours to display.

Emma Hallett (12)
Brewood CE Middle School, Brewood

I Know I Shall Return Home

As I lie on my bruised, battered torso,
shaking in agony, all I can think about is home.
Bleak summer skies, casting spells over the moor,
forests in which I roam.
Yet I am here, full of fear,
urging the night sky to come,
So I can crawl back, deep into the trenches,
my limbs limp and numb.
Watching the night fill with stars,
reminds me of memories long ago;
Stargazing, poaching, running through fields,
I'm wishing I could go.
It feels like I'm on the brink of death
while I creep through no-man's-land,
Ready to leap under barbed wire
and chase back to helping hands.
If I had a last wish it would be to go back,
for a week, for a day, for an hour,
Let my family know I'm working hard.
From battle I shall not cower,
Nor hide behind, brave, willing soldiers;
I shall stand tall amongst them all,
Telling myself, promising myself,
we will win, we will not fall.
In case they think I'm an enemy soldier,
I'm at the fence with my rifle ready,
With now one final haul to go,
I grab the metal, my body steady,
Shivering in the clear night sky,
my men come to help me,
I see a glisten of hope in their eyes,
we're winning the battle, yet at a fee;
Hundreds of our men have fallen and hundreds more to go,
Before we can come home to loved ones,
loved ones we have missed so.

Making my way back through the trenches,
I see the mud-filled pits, I do not moan,
Because I know that one day,
one day soon
I know I shall return home . . .

Scarlett Emma Rose (12)
Brewood CE Middle School, Brewood

My Future Lies In Your Hands

Would you like to see your mother die?
Would you like to be kept in a cage forever?
Would you like to see your habitat destroyed
Right in front of your eyes?
This is what my life is like,
Diggers around me, noisy, destructive,
disturbing the soil's soft slumber;
to plant palm trees for oil.

No tall trees to climb up, to use the leaves to make a night nest;
No fruit trees to find my food: mangoes, figs and lychees.
Now I cannot use the branches to swing from tree to tree,
Diggers all around me, tearing up my trees, selling the timber for money; to
plant palm trees for oil.

Chainsaws sawing through my home, everything I need to survive being
destroyed, either through burning or cutting down.
I have no space, I need my space, like any other living creature;
soon enough I'll have no home.
Please help me.

I have been taken away from my mother
and I have been illegally sold as a pet.
Caught in cages; not treated well,
so many strange faces staring at me in awe.
I don't deserve this.

I'm glad charities like the World Wildlife Foundation
are there to keep an eye on me,
to make sure I am protected.
Many places look after my brothers and sisters -
places that care for me
and make sure I have somewhere to go.

You can help me too, but adopting me through WWF.
You can also help even more
by not buying products with palm oil in.
It is in lots of things,
so make sure you check the ingredients.

With only 40,000 orang-utans like me left,
please help me.
I will very soon become extinct,
if you choose not to help me.
My future lies in your hands.

Louise Hallett (12)
Brewood CE Middle School, Brewood

Crabbit Old Man

What do you see Nurse,
What do you see?
What are thinking when you look at me?
A crabbit old man, not at all bright
A little bit deaf and losing his sight.
Sitting still and quiet, leaning back in his chair
Glasses upon his nose and grey, thin hair,
Gazes out of the window, onto the motorway
Where there once were fields, where he could play.
Accepting the changes he'd rather not see
Wasting time until dinner, lunch or tea.
That's what you see when you're looking at me
But once I was young, once I was free.
I'm not wasting time or watching space
I'm reliving my life of fun and grace.
I'm going to school, just a young child
Playing and laughing, my imagination wild.
A young man of eighteen, the love I seek
But I've found my match, a lover I meet.
I'm twenty-five now, married and have a baby
We might have another soon, just a thought, maybe.
Next I'm forty and my children are growing fast
I'll miss their childhood, however I can relax at last.
At fifty there's more children around
With smiling faces and a laughing sound.
My family and me are enjoying moments together
Yet, unfortunately, I know it won't last forever.
Things are becoming harder; my wife's passed away
And I feel older and older day after day.
My children are busy looking after their own
Consequently I've been moved to this 'old people's' home.
Now I never hear that cheerful, laughing sound
Because I've faded away into the distant background.
I feel all on my own now, like everyone's far away
And even my children can forget my birthday.
I often wonder if anyone cares
Or if I'm just equal to one of those cold winter airs.
So come over here, Nurse, talk to me

Before it's too late and you'll never see
That I'm not a crabbit old man, I'm young and I'm free
So give me that chance Nurse, let me tell you who's me.

Benjamin Hopkins (12)
Brewood CE Middle School, Brewood

My Show Pony

I love my pets, they are the best,
A pony called Page, that can be a pest.

A cream-coloured pony,
With a beautiful blond mane,
A really cheeky chappie
Who always gets the blame.

I'd love to ride him all day long,
He's fun and cheeky and sometimes strong,
I take him to the pony shows,
And everyone says, 'Oh, look how he goes.'

The ring was big, the fences were high,
I had four faults, I wonder why?
Mommy said, 'You didn't kick.'
But the wall was only a little brick!

I went again, this time I went clear
And all my friends gave a great cheer.
This time I went against the clock,
I won the class, oh what a shock!

They called my name
And I rode forward to collect my rosette,
I love my perfect pony,
He really is the best.

The day was then done,
We'd done our best
And now it's time for home
And to rest.

Matilda Stowe (11)
Brewood CE Middle School, Brewood

Child Labour

Slash! The chains are shut!
A pain in the heart and a pain in the gut,
How would you like it,
Knowing your life is slowly ending, bit by bit?
Icy tears sliding down your face,
All at a controlled yet depressing pace,
This is the reality for the children in labour,
With only family memories and moments they savour,
Your helpless hope getting less and less,
Instead of your heart filling with happiness.
How would you like it?
Whipped by day,
Whipped by night,
Only crumbs for food
And a drop to drink.
Working hard for hardly anything,
With scrapes, bruises and gashes that sting,
No one to care for you,
No one to help you,
No one to love you,
No one brave to come and save you.
How would you like it?
Slash! The chains are shut,
A pain in the heart and a pain in the gut,
Greasy, freezing tears getting more and more,
The end of your life drawing even closer,
Like your mouth reaching for an apple's core,
About to be thrown away.
How would you like it?
Think about it,
Give to charity and save lives bit by bit.

Lauren Doughty (12)
Brewood CE Middle School, Brewood

I Love Him And He Loves Me

He is an ancient fossil,
Made especially for me.
A special stone set in my heart,
I love him and he loves me.
A cuddly and soft teddy bear,
To cuddle up to when I need care.

He is battered and bruised by life,
He is a wise owl,
A chatterbox all the time,
Moaning and groaning all day and all night,
An expert driver, he's very good,
Driving all day long,
A caring and honest man,
I love him and he loves me.

He can't cook,
He will have to do,
My dad is the best,
I love him and he loves me.

Katie Jones (12)
Brewood CE Middle School, Brewood

Stay Strong

Family and friends are all around me in this time of need,
A time of grief and sadness,
But hope can still be found.

I know that we must stay strong,
Stay together through it all.

If we do this, I am sure
That we'll pull through alright.

My family and friends are so special to me
And I know that I will love them forever!

Caitlin Pagett (11)
Brewood CE Middle School, Brewood

Badgers

Like the sky at night,
Black and white,
Scampering here,
Hiding there,
Every second could be the last,
So they must beware.
Running in the dark,
Wandering alone,
Looking for shelter,
Looking for a home.

No one understands your feelings
And none hear your voice,
Where to go next,
Is your next choice.
This is still a creature,
The face of wildlife,
We should help to change
A badger's life.

Sydney Butler (12)
Brewood CE Middle School, Brewood

100 Years Ago

Were cavemen hairy
And really scary?
Were dinosaurs tall
Or really small?
I don't know,
What was the planet like
100 years ago?

Were monsters real?
What was their fave meal?
Were crocs long?
Or am I wrong?
I don't know,
What was the Earth like
100 years ago?

Could someone please tell me,
What the Earth was like
100 year ago!

Jack Rolfe (11)
Brewood CE Middle School, Brewood

Darkness

The sun goes down, the darkness rises,
I think to myself, *will the sun ever come up again?*
What about the light that makes plants grow
And the sun lighting up the sky that brings joy and laughter?

It becomes colder, a black velvet coat covers the sky,
Bringing darkness to our world.
The noisy street I walk down becomes quieter,
A white circle appears above as it replaces the sun,
What could it be?

Amber Thrya (11)
Brewood CE Middle School, Brewood

Hollywood

Driving down the boulevard
Away from LAX,
Everybody striking a pose
Gasping at Posh and Becks.

Eyes wide open at Beverley Hills,
Simon Cowell's house rocks!
Shopping bags full to the top,
A £1,000 pair of socks.

No one cares it's hailing down,
They want to see the stars,
Everybody taking shots
Of all the fancy cars.

Sadly now, it's time to go,
On the plane I fly,
Say goodbye to Hollywood,
Floating in the sky.

Emily Fisher (11)
Brewood CE Middle School, Brewood

War

A war,
Death-filled battle,
Soldiers in camouflage,
Dodging sickened bullets,
Dodging dug graves,
Wounded cries of help,
Planes, tanks, guns, weapons,
Win or lose lies in the balance,
Fight for your life,
A heart breaking descent,
One man left standing on the field,
Poppy.

Charlotte Louise Male (12)
Brewood CE Middle School, Brewood

Netball Match

The ball was in my hands
And I was shaking with fear.
Then all of a sudden, the audience started to cheer,
The ball started to slip,
I started to lose my grip.

I lunged backwards to take a shot,
Will I shoot or will I not?
I just went for it,
I watched the ball shoot up in the air

And everyone started to stare,
The ball started coming down,
My whole world turned around,
The ball went through the net.

I guess the boys had lost their bet!
Everyone started chanting my name,
As we won the championship game.

Aimee Clemson (11)
Brewood CE Middle School, Brewood

War

Soldiers do all they can
To fight against the Taliban.

As their parents weep and cry
Their children slowly die.

Is this really fair?
Do they really care?

Soldier after soldier fell,
Surely that must feel like Hell?

So if you really care,
Let's pull our soldiers out of there!

Adam Osbourne (12) & Patrick Marshall (12)
Brewood CE Middle School, Brewood

Netball Match

Standing there with the ball in my hands,
Fans screaming and shouting in the stands.
My team were nearly halfway there,
I tensed up as the ball flew in the air.

And yes, the ball went in,
My teammates were staring with a grin.
'Come on, let's win,' shouted Perton's keeper,
I really hope we don't get beaten.

As the match went on I scraped back my hair,
I was not looking forward to watching in despair.
The ball was travelling faster than Formula 1,
I really hoped we would be number one.

Reflecting back, faster than ever,
Jess passed the ball back to Heather,
Yes, the torture had ended,
The buzzer had sounded.

Amy White (11)
Brewood CE Middle School, Brewood

My Birthday

(Dedicated to my super mom)

The best time of year is when my birthday is here,
With lots of things to do and spend the day with you.

Spreading love and laughter is what I do best,
I hope that you think I'm better than all the rest.

So when my birthday is done and the fun has gone,
Just remember my birthday is so special because you are there,
And the best thing about it is you, Mom!

Casey Whittingham (11)
Brewood CE Middle School, Brewood

War

Sitting in the trenches, waiting for that call,
Will I survive, or will I fall?
Shells being fired all around,
We hit an enemy soldier - he falls to the ground.

The order is given so I jump out and run,
Eventually I stop . . . then raise my gun.
I fire my bullets, they fly through the air,
Silently, I say a prayer.

An explosion behind knocks me off my feet,
Lay on the ground I hear my heart beat.
I stay still, knowing I will die,
Is this the spot in which I will forever lie?

A fellow comrade helps me to stand,
I shall not die in no-man's-land.
We search the battlefield for all who survive,
I must be blessed because I'm alive.

Jake Glynn (12)
Brewood CE Middle School, Brewood

Mean A Lot To You

Families are important
They help you every day
Through the ups and downs in your life
Guide you through your troubles and strife
Their cuddles are warm and cosy
They make us feel safe and cared for
Friends are just as special too
They'll always mean a lot to you!

Katie Chidlow, Caitlin Pagett & Lucy Woodhouse (11)
Brewood CE Middle School, Brewood

War Is A Light Shining

There was gunfire all around,
Suddenly, there was no sound,
I thought all of my team had gone,
It turns out they were stunned by a bomb.
There was a shelter nearby,
We entered it and I started to cry.
All the deaths I've seen are uncountable,
We would take a bullet to save one another's life,
That's not always the case.
Every morning I wake up, thinking
This could be the end.
What keeps me going is the fact
That I'm fighting for my Queen, country and friends.
I saw a light shining above,
It reminded me of my true love,
It won't be long now until I'm home
Until then I'll feel alone.

Jack Smith (11)
Brewood CE Middle School, Brewood

Friendship

If you smile every day
People will love you all the way.
And every time you give a smile
They will think of you for a while.
If they do not smile back,
You will find it is friendship they lack.
When you look back you will see,
The friendship that lies between you and me.

Alice Nightingale (11)
Brewood CE Middle School, Brewood

Goodbye

Too soon you left in all that pain,
I miss that laugh I'll not hear again.
You made me laugh, you made me cry,
I wish you didn't have to die.

A poem, a memory, a tear we all share,
The lights on stage for you no longer glare.
Your hour upon the stage you did strut,
But all that's left of your song is white soot.

I know it's time for you to go,
What's left of you down the cliff we'll throw.
Handful by handful, downwards you fall,
Sweeping down the cliff to a gull's call.

Patterns of dust downward swirl to the sea,
Down, down, the cliff you go as we set you free.

Kate Langford (12)
Brewood CE Middle School, Brewood

Black

Broken-hearted, kills love between two,
Hatred, fiery rage, destroying all around me.
Anger pushes you over the edge,
Emotion's a flood of good or bad,
Could be happy, could be sad.
Meaningless, yanks you far beyond help,
Alone, cuts you off from anything else.
Doubt gets into your soul,
Turns it into a huge black hole,
Forever here to stay you are here for evermore,
Revenge, it is like a poison,
Keeps you going until you are completely taken,
Tears and cries, they sadden you,
Make you slowly die.

Kristian Milligan (12)
Brewood CE Middle School, Brewood

44

War Is Something That Should Never Occur

English soldiers creep across the field,
Our formation is as safe as a shield.
From nowhere gunfire suddenly starts,
My squadron have trembling hearts.
My family keep me going strong,
We're all commanded to move along.
We each throw a murderous hand grenade,
The other side don't seem afraid.
Then they release a nuclear bomb,
Now nearly all my friends are gone.
There is a lot of radiation,
It causes absolute devastation.

War is something that should never occur,
We all want peace - that's what we'd prefer.

Michael Lunn (11)
Brewood CE Middle School, Brewood

Friends

Friends stick together forever,
They will never break up, no never.
They win together, lose together,
Smile together and fight the blues together.
Friends stick together forever,
They will never break up, no never.
When you are with your friends they make you smile,
You know that life is worthwhile.
Friends cheer you up when you are down,
Most good friends deserve a crown.
Friends are always there for you through thick and thin,
If you play games with your friends it doesn't matter if you win.
Friends are together forever,
They will never break up, no never!

Lily Wilkes (11)
Brewood CE Middle School, Brewood

The Night Of Halloween

About six o'clock at night,
Children dress up to give people a nasty fright.

They knock on doors saying, 'Trick or treat?'
Just to get something tasty and sweet.

The older people stick up posters saying,
'Sorry, no trick or treating here.'
To make sure no witches nor skeletons come near.

Pumpkins sit in the door frame, with bright, yellow light,
The little children sit and carve, to their own delight.

Now can you see what I see?
A scary and spooky night,
With a reward of sweets for free!

Jodie Ryan (12)
Brewood CE Middle School, Brewood

Afghanistan

Many lives are lost,
Is it worth the cost?
While mothers weep,
Lives are cheap.
As they're using an MP5,
Soldiers are based in a dive.
In the NAAFI chips are fried,
In no-man's-land people died.
Still the Taliban do hide.
There are bullets everywhere,
You hope they only brush your hair,
Because if they hit your head
You are dead.

Jack Poade (11)
Brewood CE Middle School, Brewood

I Love Her . . .

I love her when she comforts me when I am down.
I even love her when she has a frown.
I love her when she feeds my belly,
I love her when she lets me watch the telly.

I love her when she takes me out,
I even love her when she starts to shout.
I love her when she gives me a hug,
I love her when she looks after me when I have a bug.

I love her when she feeds me tea,
I love her when she tickles me,
I love her when she's just herself,
Of course, it's my mom.

Sophie Coss (11)
Brewood CE Middle School, Brewood

The Shark

When I went on holiday
You will never guess what I saw.
It was a great white shark,
Lurking on the sea floor.

I quickly ran away,
To get to my mom and dad
And when I got back
I was really mad.

The shark had disappeared,
Into the open sea,
I was really sad,
Because no one would believe me!

Hayden Wingfield (11)
Brewood CE Middle School, Brewood

My Mom

My mom is the best,
Better than the rest,
Being funny wherever she goes,
She always lets it show.
I love my mom a lot,
She always gives a lot.

She gets through everything,
I don't know how she does it,
Spending time washing, cleaning
And never stops believing.
That's my mom
And she's the best in the world!

Molly Pinson (12)
Brewood CE Middle School, Brewood

My Special Grandad

G reat listener to people
R espectful in so many ways
A lways kind to people
N ickname, 'The Flying Dutchman'
D ancer he was in his prime
A n excellent artist, painting he prefers
D usting off his bicycle, dreaming of his fast days.

Ralph Allard-Blackshaw (12)
Brewood CE Middle School, Brewood

A Friend Is . . .

F orever there for you
R eally fun
I nteresting
E xciting
N ever lets you feel left out
D ependable
S pecial.

Hannah Groom (11)
Brewood CE Middle School, Brewood

Nature

The ocean is a soft, sweet start.
Trees tough as boots in the rumbling rain.
Animals, all sizes and shapes gather groups of gooseberries.
Darkness drowns us with droopy, dreadful sorrow.
Water, wet and wild, with weird fun ad happiness.
This world is a funny, fumbling thing.
Thanks for making a funny, fumbling thing, everybody!

Katie Riley (11)
Brewood CE Middle School, Brewood

What Matters To Me

Rugby
I woke up, knowing it was match day,
Hoping their best players were away.
Got up to have a shower, thinking how we were going to play.
Putting on the kit, feeling the pride,
Knowing you could win,
But one mistake could take victory away,
Like life for a healthy person.
Pulling up the socks, putting on the top,
The track suit and believing in the victory,
The happiness you feel.
Seeing your team jump with excitement,
But remembering the defeat last time.
Walking away with heads down,
An injured soldier.
Getting in the car, silence!
Nothing to be said.
Driving up the motorway,
Trying to remember the moves and the tactics.
The current players to watch out for.
The one thing your dad says, 'Smash them!'
Getting out the car, seeing the opposition,
Eyeing up your number,
Knowing if you tackle him hard he will never come back.
Then, seeing your team's tactics in the changing room.
Then running out onto the park,
Kicking, handling and stretching.
Getting onto the team huddle,
Captain telling you to be your best,
Play hard but fair and shocking laughs,
But you could see how much he wanted to win.
The captain called our kick,
I got the ball, I kicked off,
Their player caught it then . . .

Ben Phillips (13)
Bromsgrove School, Bromsgrove

What Matters To Me

What matters to me?
What do you think it could be?
Presents, clothes, books or money?
Oh please, don't be funny!
All that matters to me is
My family and friends.
They are like a rare diamond
Which you can't find on every island.
They protect you every second,
When I'm feeling bad
Or someone made me mad.
They always try to help me,
A solution they can often see,
Once I said we will be friends forever,
Separated we can never be.
Clap, clap! I heard,
I turned and saw a little bird,
Lost in the dark forest,
It broke its friend's trust
That's why they left him alone,
Far, far away from home.
Does a friendship last forever?
The answer is no, however
Friends are like a knife,
Very useful sometimes in life.
But they can cut deep
Even if you are asleep.
The trust you should never lose,
Try to see their views.
I told you what matters to me,
Now you feel completely free
To write about yourself.

Nikol Grigorova (14)
Bromsgrove School, Bromsgrove

Reading

Reading is watching your mind,
It can give the imagination of the blind.

Reading brings you dreams,
So various are the themes.

Reading makes you think, *what if . . .?*
Macbeth, Romeo and Juliet or Henry V.

Reading will give you a blackened, charred world full of savages,
Or sunlit meadow, or a field full of cabbages.

A world where around every corner lies danger,
Or sweet Jesus in a manger.

Reading can be a world where it is kill or be killed,
Where you can laugh, cry or be thrilled.

Reading brings death in every gruesome aspect,
Or Sherlock Holmes with crimes to detect.

Reading can make you someone other than you,
A Christian, Muslim or Jew.

Reading can change your world in so many ways,
Where minutes turn to hours and hours to days.

Reading can transport you back to Victorian times,
Before Eminem was making rhymes.

What will the next book bring?
The rise of a peasant or the fall of a king?

Richard Armstrong (13)
Bromsgrove School, Bromsgrove

Free Kick

He put it down
On the surface ground
He took a step back
He looked at his pack
He gave a nod
They gave a smile
He looked at the crowd
They were shouting and screaming
It was like the ball was shouting at them
He was heavy, he was warmed up, he was ready
He rushed to the ball
And took his step next to the ball
Then with his free leg he swung it
Hit the ball hard, with incredible speed
Then there was silence, as the ball
Was swerving and cutting through the air
When it hit the net, immediately
The crowd cheered
He ran to the ball as he was sliding
He laughed and felt the air pressure of his fellow friends
The smell of grass went up his nose
Victory was easily pushed in his pockets

They weren't losers
They weren't quitters
They were winners!

Uchan Thapa (13)
Bromsgrove School, Bromsgrove

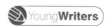
What Matters To Me - Hockey

The energy before the start,
Everyone buzzing and excited,
Ready to win again.
We all jump into position,
Whistle blows and we start.
The sound of the ball
Whizzing onto your stick,
Whoosh, slap, whoosh, slap!
You feel the vibration through your fingers
When you hit the ball
And know if you have made a good shot.
The sound of the backboard,
When the ball sprints over the line and past the goalie,
Straight into the goal.
Everyone you know and love
Shouting you on,
Cheering for you to get a goal,
To win yet another match.
The final whistle blows
And you scream and shout,
As you know you have won.
You taste victory in the air
And everyone relaxes.
We've won and the game is over . . .

Sophie Swatkins (13)
Bromsgrove School, Bromsgrove

What Matters To Me

The boot of the ball
The hefty ping
The noise in the crowd
The whistle

The pressure
The excitement
The fear
The break

The white line metres away
Two men to beat
Quick thinking
Look right and left

The pass
The hope
The cheers
The celebrations

The clapping
The commentator
The announcements
The big final

This is rugby!

Harry Sebastian Broom (13)
Bromsgrove School, Bromsgrove

The Samaritan

As he walked to the corner of the alleyway,
he saw three hooded youths,
Shouting and pushing two younger boys that he knew.
In his mind he knew he could not just walk away
from what he'd seen,
He pictured his younger brother there and decided to intervene.
He ran up to the hooded boys, asking, 'What's up?'
'Shut up, brehh,' one of them said, grabbing him by the hair
and he thrust a sharp metal object into the Samaritan.
Then the three ruthless youths ran as if it were a marathon.
All angry and deluded, they cried, 'Next time Blud, you get shooted.'
He fell to the floor, crying out in pain,
He only wished to see his mom before the blood left his brain.
A lady appeared over him, shocked at the sight,
'I'm a nurse,' she said, 'It will be better by tonight.'
The young boy just about made it to hospital fine,
But he sadly passed away later that night.
But if it wasn't for that woman and the first aid she applied,
The boy wouldn't have had a chance to see his mom before he died.
It's because he was a Good Samaritan that God answered his cries,
Otherwise he would have never again looked into his mother's eyes.
So the next time you see an injustice, don't avoid it,
Because the boy was 16 and didn't deserve it.

Ryan Byrne (14)
Bromsgrove School, Bromsgrove

What Matters To Me -
Beauty - The Morning Mist

The morning mist engulfs the terrain,
It hangs like a heavy, grey blanket over the Earth
and hides all from view.
Skeletal black trees protrude from shadows,
They are bony, taloned creatures that scratch and wound the sky,
They make it bleed,
They make it cry,
Ribbons of red stain the firmament and tears of pain
fall from the heavens.

As I meander through the chill, moist atmosphere, my clothes absorb the dampness
My garments cling to my limbs and make me shiver.
My passing, leaves marks imprinted on the sodden turf,
and then the transformation.
The warming, golden rays of the sun illuminate the azure.
Songs of ecstatic birds announce the dawn.
They herald the coming day.

The frigid night is pushed aside,
Shards of sunlight dapple my skin and melt away the night.
The mist, thick as it was, begins to depart.

Yash Shanghavi (13)
Bromsgrove School, Bromsgrove

What Matters To Me - Water

Water is your personal doctor,
When you feel feverish it's there to soothe you down.
When you boil up inside it's there to melt your anger,
When your throat burns, water will be there.

Water is a holy element, blessed by the gods,
Have you seen the way it glints in the sun?
Have you heard it lapping like a dog, longing for attention?
This is not just water, it's holy water.

Water can also hear God's thoughts,
It can sense when God is sad,
When God is sad the world cries, the heavens pelt us with droplets
And then everybody cries, water links God's feelings with you.

Water can also suspend you from the ground, making you free,
When you are on land you are in control,
When you are in the sea, water takes control, you are at its mercy,
Water can do anything to you
and you wouldn't be able to do anything.

However, water has made its own enemy, listen . . .
When the great waves hit rock, can you hear the roar?
That is the sound of two great foes in battle
And that battle will continue for centuries.

Matthew Jones (13)
Bromsgrove School, Bromsgrove

The Land Where I Am Free

When summer's high the bluebells rise
Like an ocean over the meadow
Where only the trees break their waves
And all you can hear is the breeze

Sitting on the fallen oak, gazing over the bay
The blues, purples and greens all wonders for me to see
With light breaking through cloudy treetops
Like shadows falling heavily on my shimmering sea

Ships sailing happily, through the purple maze
Barking blissfully round and round, almost on top of me
And flying above, aimlessly, adoring all he sees
The dog's god in paradise, smiling cheerfully

A place to hide inside my world
Where only I know the way
Secrets popping in and out
The land where I am free

A glimmering gem on the ground
Blissfully unaware of what they've found
Curiously staring at the key
Not knowing what it means to me.

Robert Chapman (14)
Bromsgrove School, Bromsgrove

What Matters To Me

We charge like bulls onto the pitch
Ready and raring to go.
Our minds are set on winning,
As the whistle goes
The cheers from the crowd, shouting like animals,
You feel the taste of victory.
Whoosh! As the ball is struck and everybody waits and hopes,
Then finally the ball goes into the back of the net,
Your eyes glow with glee.

The feeling when you have a good shot,
Or skill someone
And you know your part of the plot,
Fighting for winning the cup.
As the final whistle goes the ambition in our faces,
We hear the tension raising high,
As the time passes by.

The whistle goes, our time is up,
We win, we cheer and scream,
We lose, we learn.
Oh the fanatic of football!

Poppy Jones (14)
Bromsgrove School, Bromsgrove

What Matters A Lot To Me

With all my heart I proudly say
I love my family every day
I love my mum
Just like the sun
And both my brothers
Dad and Eve
If someone asks me
'Are you bored?' I
Will answer, 'No. I
Have just done some sport.'

I go to every single
Trip to the zoo, so
I can look at Kienguru!
I have to tell you
That I mess round
And play all day
Just like they do.

I love my friends
And this is how
The poem ends.

Sofya Syskova (13)
Bromsgrove School, Bromsgrove

What Matters To Me

One against the world.
People shunt the game like beggars in the street.
You need skill like a bird diving for its prey.
I swing, swing until can swing no more.
The mind must be like a still pool
In the moonlight
A fraction out can make all the difference
The perfect strike will send the ball flying
Like a bullet out of a gun
Soaring through the air like a majestic eagle
Like a sculptor, a golfer must pay attention
To the finest detail to be the best
Patience, patience is the key
The key to the door of victory
Without the key you will be locked out
When the final putt sinks
You know your job is done.

Sam Bellamy (13)
Bromsgrove School, Bromsgrove

What Matters To Me

What matters to me . . .
To ride or not to ride,
What a stupid question!
On a beautiful summer's day
The crop fields spread through
The land like there's no end,
Peaceful wind brushes through the trees,
Their whinnies are a sound of freedom,
Mounting my horse, we gallop through the wind as one.
Moving through the crops,
Both of us together is like touching energy.

Rosie Louise Thompson (14)
Bromsgrove School, Bromsgrove

Music

Music is the only thing that matters to me,
It's soothing to hear, like waves from the sea.
My favourite three types are reggae, pop and rap,
All of which you can join in with and perhaps clap.

All music can make you sad or happy,
As every song tends to have a story,
Whether it's live in a stadium or a recording,
There's a ghostly silence of people listening.

All artists are so glad when they're done,
Especially if every note's to perfection,
Music's the only thing that matters to me,
As it's so unpredictable what the next song may be.

Alex Griffiths (14)
Bromsgrove School, Bromsgrove

It Doesn't Matter Jack

How dare you push him across the playground
And call him names like that!
To a boy who hasn't done anything wrong.
He's different, so what?
Who decides what's normal or not?
He's normal to me, that's what matters,
He was born that way.
So when you push him across the playground
And call him names,
Just think, you could have been born that way.

Jasmin Steer (14)
Caistor Yarborough School, Caistor

Socks

When I have to choose one pair of socks,
I have a bit of a problem.
Black ones, white ones, dull ones, bright ones,
Ones with stripes or dots?
Pink socks, blue socks,
Old socks, new socks?
Even socks with lollipops!

Plain socks for school,
Cake socks are cool!
Baby socks are really small,
I've socks for each day of the week, month and year,
I've even socks for standing here!

Which socks to wear?
Do I really care?
Or maybe I'll leave my feet bare!
Perhaps I'll wear my old, thick pair?
Oh no, they're not there!

My wardrobe's a sock pick 'n' mix,
Which pair to choose?
'Please be quick!'
I ruthlessly throw socks around,
A sea of socks is on the ground.

Then, gleaming there, like a pot of gold,
One pair of socks, not new, not old,
My red pair, with polka dots,
They're my favourite of all my socks!
I slump to the ground, finally
I grasp my socks only to see . . .

There's a great big, gaping hole,
Slitted along the sole,
I growl in anger and in pain,
I suppose that I'll just have to wear
The pair I wore last week, again.

Lucy Adams (12)
Campion School, Bugbrooke

Bullying

I'm so upset
I can't go on
I want to hide
They made me cry

The followed me home
They tripped me up
They took my books
They ripped them up

I felt trapped
I felt alone
I couldn't cope
I was on my own

I didn't tell
I'm sorry Mum
I'm sorry Dad
Hope you understand
It was really bad

The hurt was too much
I couldn't go on
As well as the pain
I would have gone insane.

Lucy Dickens (13)
Campion School, Bugbrooke

What Matters To Me

Music
    Without it herself or himself or itself wouldn't be themselves or
    maybe not anything at all.
Understanding
    When I listen to music I know how I feel
    The things that seem unreal become so real
    As the newest songs reveal to be in the top ten
Silence
    I hate silence, I prefer the music flowing between my ears
    And then my body reacts to what it hears
    As if it's abstract sounds
Intelligence
    Music makes me smarter . . .
    Temporarily of course
    I like when a new song is being endorsed
Creative
    Having no boundaries
    Makes it impossible to be wrong
    And it doesn't matter what you like, rock, pop, metal, jazz,
    Classical, rap or indie, everyone's opinions are strong.

    Music is important to me.

Sarah Waterhouse (11)
Campion School, Bugbrooke

For Mark

(Miss you so much, will never forget you!)

Life takes away many precious things
If we were all angels it would take away our wings
But now it has taken someone deep in our hearts
And many of us have just fallen apart
Mark was a close friend to everyone
A boy lost in his music, guitar and song
Gone like that, without any warning
Some of his close ones are still sadly in mourning
The happiest lad of us all
We just can't believe he took the fall
Now we know he's gone up to a different place
Somewhere without matters of size, style or race
He has gone from our clutches, holding on tight
And we pray for him back with all of our might
And so the wonderful boy with the wacky hair
Rest in peace Mark Tanton, we will always care.

Evie Russell (14)
Campion School, Bugbrooke

Wintertime

W inter is the ice on the roads.
 I nside the fire is blazing, but it's no match for the cold.
 N ear the pond the grass has gone white.
 T hen it starts to snow.
 E ars are as cold as ice lollies.
 R ivers are frozen like ice rinks.
 T rees are topped with snow.
 I n the garden the hedgehogs are hibernating.
 M y nose is as blue as the sky.
 E ven though it's so c-cold, you still go outside.

Frazer Dickens (11)
Campion School, Bugbrooke

War

Why do you do it?
Do you find it fun?
Killing and harming everyone
Causing pain and devastation
Leaving trails of disdain
Rivers flowing red, blood-red
Blood of people you fought, dead

I ask you again, why?
Can I persuade you?
No?
Help heal rather than harm
And love instead of hate
Send my message to the world
Please cause much less pain.

Sarah Boyle (13)
Campion School, Bugbrooke

Teenagers

We're not all vandals, we're not all bad,
We're not all violent, we're not all mad,
We're not all horrible, we're not all cheap,
We're not all in gangs, not everyone's words are *beep!*

We don't all bunk off school, we don't all get bad grades,
We don't all think we're cool, we don't all let relationships fade,
We don't all wander around aimlessly, we don't all carry knives,
We don't all hate our family, we just want to live our lives!

Holly Botterill (13)
Campion School, Bugbrooke

The Predator

I can't feel my head,
I can't feel my toes,
I feel the blood running down my nose,
I hear it again,
The menacing growl,
From which I fearfully hid when the beast started to prowl,
It's smashing through tables, cupboards and doors,
It's getting closer and starting to roar,
I close my eyes and count to three,
Wishing there was somewhere, anywhere else that I could be,
But that's not how it goes,
He comes after me . . .
I can no longer count, one, two, three,
And now I'm not there
And I see him stare
Into the mist of utter despair,
Sitting in his cell,
Lonesome and cold,
Having to stay until he is dying and old,
If he hadn't hunted,
Thrashed out and killed,
Maybe we would have been happy . . .
But now we never will.

Harriet Burns (14)
Leek High Specialist Technology School, Leek

War

It spills into the peaceful town,
Then towards the hill it comes tumbling down.
Moving fast, burning, rolling, killing,
No matter what it keeps on spilling.

As it smoulders, destroys and causes pain,
Running swiftly through the rain
And as it comes, a cry for help,
Innocent people starting to yelp.

Tears of blood, pain and sorrow,
The spill has a heart that's hollow,
As the burning fire of death comes fast,
Many years, for this will last.

Once young people had a dream,
Now their life is a silent scream
As this spillage turned you raw,
The fiery feeling of fighting war.

Robert Alexander (13)
Leek High Specialist Technology School, Leek

What Matters To Me

My family is important in my life
I can see them day and night
They'll be there for me all the time
They'll always be mine

My friends are really kind and awesome
They are fun to play with when I'm all alone
And sometimes I can call them on the phone

My health is important in my life
I should be careful all the time
I should make it great and nice
Live your life the best you can!

John Llanes (11)
New Mills School, New Mills

Winter

Having snowball fights will all my friends,
Skidding on the ice, that's fun too,
Building snowmen on the street,
Sledging down the big hills,
Watching the snow fall
Through my window,
Ice cold hands,
Feet too,
Fun!

Amy Toft (12)
New Mills School, New Mills

The Bullies

Whatever happened
To people being treated fairly?
Now all you hear is
'Miss! He hurt me!'

I tried to fit in
I tried, I really did!
But people started hurting me
So most of the time I hid

I spent most of my life in hiding
And now it's time to fight back
Not just at health and safety
But at those kids who did attack

Me, I know that it is wrong
I know I shouldn't fight
But they were so horrid
So it's time to set things right

'Oi,' I said to them
'I owe you something'
'Oh, we know that,'
One of them said with a grin

I walked right up to them
When no one ever would
'You've bullied me my whole life
And I know you're up to no good!

You always used to do this,'
I said, tears streaming down my face
'You were horrid, you were mean
And you're a disgrace!

But that's not now
Now is when we fight.
But for others not just me
I'm going to set things right.'

So I hit and I slapped
And I kicked harder than anything
And after five minutes

They were all crying

They tried to fight back
So I hit them with a pail
And I scratched them
With my fake nails

Now they act like servants
They replaced the money they stole
They help me with my homework
And do as they are told

They're never horrid now
They are always kind
And their parents have thanked me
Loads of times.

Jessica Hipson (13)
New Mills School, New Mills

Music Means A Lot To Me

Dance music, pop music, R 'n' B,
Beyoncé, Miley, The Saturdays,
I listen to music on my stereo,
No one can beat Jason Derulo.

'Just Dance', by Lady Gaga is a great track,
'The Promise', by Girls Aloud always takes me back,
I always want to know who is in the charts,
Music's forever been in my heart.

It cheers me up when I'm feeling down,
It picks me up off the ground;
Lyrics sometimes fit your situation,
Music often helps control my emotions.

I don't know what I'd do if music was gone,
It's important to (mainly) everyone;
Dancing to the beat, singing along,
What is your favourite song?

Katie Jones (13)
New Mills School, New Mills

The Things That Matter To me

The things that matter to me . . .
Well, there are a lot of things that turn my head,
For one thing, good music and cellos and food,
But for baked beans I wouldn't turn a hair.

But the thing I love most,
Well you might not agree,
But my opinion is that pets matter most.

I have a guinea pig, called Ollie,
I used to have a hamster, called Hamish,
I have three fish, called Bubbles, Jo and Zoe,
You may think they're strange names for fish.

Some other things also matter,
Including family and friends and technology,
World issues, like the credit crunch,
Don't really have a place in me.

But cellos are really top notch,
In my view, but maybe not yours,
I wouldn't play any other instrument than the most regal of strings.

I know that is a lot of things,
But overall everything matters to me,
(Except baked beans).

Anna Bagnall (11)
New Mills School, New Mills

Memories

Memories are thoughts that you will treasure forever
And remind you of loved ones and the times you shared together.
Some make you feel happy
Some make you feel sad
And others give you moments that made you feel glad.

Memories are like treasures inside your mind,
That once opened can fill you with thoughts of inspiration,
They make you laugh
They make you cry
And often make you wonder why.

Memories are like gems,
That once found you hold on to forever,
They make you remember the good times,
The bad times
And things you go through in everyday life.

Memories are like your first Christmas present,
The more you unfold
The more you discover,
Often the glimpse of disappointment,
But mostly the glimpse of excitement.

The amazing thing about memories
Is that you can always look back on them for help and advice.
They flicker inside your mind
And take you somewhere far away.
Then you find yourself smiling at that one special day.

Memories can also have their faults,
Sometimes they fade,
Get pushed into the shade
And become shadows amongst the darkness.
But even though you may forget
It's often time you will regret.

So even though they be good or bad,
They are always going to be up there, hidden in your mind.
Moments of happiness
And pictures of sorrow
Are kept within the heart

:5

Poems From The Midlands

And others are kept in the dark.
But they will last you a lifetime
And stick with you
Forever.

Kimberley Scholes (13)
New Mills School, New Mills

What Matters To Me

Sport matters to me, because it's fun and it's healthy,
With mates like mine you don't need to be wealthy.
I like to play football and cricket,
But when I'm at the crease you aren't touching my wicket.

Family matters to me,
Even my brother,
I'll even spare the time
For my stressy old mother.

I like to play my PlayStation Three,
Some people play war games, but they're not for me,
The ones I play are footy games and cricket,
If you try to make me play COD, I'll tell you where to stick it.

I like Manchester United,
They're my favourite team,
Rooney, Giggs and Fergie,
They matter to me.

When I'm writing this poem,
I'm sitting with my mates,
Talking about which team each of us hates.
That's what matters to me.

Daniel Palmer (12)
New Mills School, New Mills

My Dog, Jess

Jess was my best friend
But when she went
I knew she was sent
To the world ahead

I loved taking her on walks
Sometimes it hurt her paws
And I hoped I didn't cause
A bad infection

Her favourite food was lasagne
She always ate it all
Just like me and my dad Paul
She loved it to bits

I miss Jess a lot
She mattered to me so much
She really loved a clutch
From me

But I am all right
Because I have Fudge
She always gives me a budge
To see if I am OK.

Danielle Allsop (11)
New Mills School, New Mills

The Things In The World

The sky is blue
The grass is green
Clouds are grey
But sadly, some things are mean

Like terrorists
And murderers
But I don't think about them
I think about these

Like teachers
And doctors
And people who
Help others

Maybe people who help the country
The navy, the army
The air force
But there are others who are less violent

The chefs, the cleaners
The vicars, the lawyers
And the football players
And the people who are beside us.

Harry Hughes (12)
New Mills School, New Mills

Molly, The Dog

M olly, my auntie's dog passed away a few days ago
O ur family is very upset
L ovely, big Newfoundland dog
L ively, but as she got older started to get poorly
Y et why did she have to die?

Nicole Hardy (12)
New Mills School, New Mills

Bella's Disaster

My pet Bella, stroked by my hand
The only one I could understand
After a bang erupts from the road
A lie by Mum I had been told

The end of the day, back at home
Mum breaks the news, I was alone
No cute tabby to play with me
She's at the vet instead of being free

A few weeks later, still upset
But I hadn't heard the full story yet
Mum and Dad will go their separate ways
And they are still like that today

Although Bella is now free
She's not with our family
Mum's old friend took her in
Life without Bella's really dim

I know Bella's safe and sound
But by me she'll never be found
It feels there's anything I would ask her
Still feel lost after Bella's disaster.

Lucy Ann Thorp (13)
New Mills School, New Mills

The City

In the city the buildings so high.
The busy streets and the birds that fly.
The central block,
Full of shops,
The fountain in the middle,
The train station and the stop.
The city's what matters to me!

Molly Witty (12)
New Mills School, New Mills

You're That One Special Person

You make me feel special,
I know that you care,
It makes my heart pound
As I know that you're there.
When you're upset,
When you're sat there all alone,
I can tell you're unhappy,
I can tell by your tone.
If we fall out
And you hate me and lie,
It still wouldn't matter,
But I would still want to try.
It's not the way you dress,
It's not the person you're pretending to be,
It's your smile and personality,
That's all that matters to me.

As you're the one special person,
I think about you all the time,
You mean the world to me
And I'm so glad you're mine.

Rosie Whitehead (12)
New Mills School, New Mills

If

If luck were a minute, I'd send you an hour,
If hope was a raindrop, I'd send you a shower,
If love was a tear, I'd send you a sea,
If you need a friend, you'll always have me.

If happiness was a candle, I'd send you a fire,
If song makes you smile, I'd send you a choir,
If memories make you laugh, I'll remind you of them all,
If I'm with you, I know I'll never fall.

Charlie Parker (12)
New Mills School, New Mills

Across The Globe

I live at home, in a house of bricks,
Across the globe a house of sticks.

I'm sitting, playing on my iPod Touch,
Across the globe a child without much!

I leave for school with all my books,
Across the globe is filled with crooks.

I became ill with little more than a sneeze,
Across the globe a child with disease.

School is part of my day to day life,
Across the globe a child accustomed to knives.

Food isn't scarce and so easily retrieved,
Across the globe full isn't achieved!

I go to sleep without a thought in my head,
Across the globe a child longing to be fed!

I hear on the news about a quake,
Across the globe a child won't wake!

Philippa Loftus (13)
New Mills School, New Mills

Hunter

It hunts and curls its tail
As it sees its prey
It ducks low and waits, waits
Until it gets closer, closer
And pounces at thirty miles per hour
The prey doesn't stand a chance

It brings back its prey
To its owner, wanting to get praised for its hard work
But the owner sighs that the mess needs cleaning
Waiting till dawn comes so it can start hunting again.

Alex Smiles (12)
New Mills School, New Mills

What Matters To Me

My family matters to me,
They are always there for me,
They are a part of my life,
They make me feel better.

My Xbox matters to me,
It's fun to play,
New games are excellent,
It is so cool.

My friends matter to me,
They cheer me up,
They give and lend you stuff,
They make you laugh.

Football matters to me,
It's an exciting sport,
It's full of entertainment,
It is amusing.

They are all awesome to me.

Jack Stang (12)
New Mills School, New Mills

What Matters To Me

My dad, mum, sister and brother mean a lot to me,
So I don't feel lonely,
They make me feel happy.

My pets are someone to talk to when I am feeling down,
Even though they don't talk back,
But still make me feel happy and over the moon.

My friends always cheer me up when I'm sad,
They make me laugh and will always be there for me.

These are the things that truly matter to me!

Charlotte Wilson (12)
New Mills School, New Mills

84

My Family And Friends Are My World

What matters to me is,
They're here in a whizz,
My family and friends are my world.

We argue, gossip and laugh,
Walking down the school path,
But I wouldn't change a thing.

My dad cooks tea,
Me and my sister play on the Wii,
My mum just looks and laughs.

I wanted a dog,
They'd prefer a frog,
But they eventually gave in.

We'd stay up till three
Carve our names on a tree
I love them all so much.

Oh, my family and friends are my world.

Lauren Garlick (13)
New Mills School, New Mills

Families

F amilies are always there for you
A lways there when you need a helping hand
M ums are a best friend
I like my family, we are like an elastic band
L ove is always there
Y ou're there for me and I'm there for you.

Chloe Green (12)
New Mills School, New Mills

YoungWriters

What Matters To Me

My family matters to me,
They are part of my life,
I don't wish to be alone,
They love and care for me.

My friends matter to me,
They're very special people,
They will be in my heart forever,
They cheer me up when I'm down.

Children matter to me,
I wonder how they will grow up
And I wonder what they will look like,
But mainly who they are not what they are.

The environment matters to me,
It's a beautiful place,
There is so much to see,
In such little time.

Jonathan Swindells (12)
New Mills School, New Mills

My Mum

She is beautiful,
She is the best,
She is helpful,
Like all the rest.

She loves me,
I love her,
She is a twinkling star.

She's good at listening,
It's like her job,
Even though she's embarrassing,
She is never in the wrong.

Sophie Taylor (12)
New Mills School, New Mills

86

What Matters To Me

My family matters to me,
They make me smile and they make my tea,
My family matters to me,
They're all I've wanted them to be.

My friends matter to me,
They fill me up with glee,
My friends matter to me,
Sometimes they're over for tea.

My dog matters to me,
Sometimes he sits on my knee,
My dog matters to me,
I take him out for a wee.

My cat matters to me,
He likes to eat meat,
My cat matters to me,
He likes it when he gets his treat.

Danielle Graham (12)
New Mills School, New Mills

What Matters To Me

My family matters to me because they are caring
And they are always there for me, so I'm not alone.

My friends matter to me, they cheer me up when I'm sad
And they talk to me and stand by me.

Football matters to me because it keeps me from being bored,
I play football all the time with my dad and brother.

Music matters to me, because when I'm upset I listen to my iPod
Or go into to my room and listen to CDs.

Pets matter to me, because I like to look after them
And play with them, I used to have a pet hamster called Carly.

Amy Stanton (11)
New Mills School, New Mills

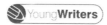

What Matters To Me

W alking with my aunty
H aving a football net to play in
A t a Sky Fun Day with my family
T he fact I have free Sky TV

M y family
A great lot of friends
T he subjects at school, especially DT
T he holidays in Turkey
E ating spaghetti Bolognaise
R eading Michael Symons books
S troking my pet mouse

T rips to the cinema
O r bike riding with my dad

M y fish of which there are many
E ven though I have to feed them.

Tom Hall (11)
New Mills School, New Mills

My Feelings

You can like me or not,
Whatever you want to think,
I try my best every day
To impress you.
I don't know what I have done wrong,
It's just not the same anymore,
I loved you once, but no, not anymore.
I don't care what you look like, it's the way you are to me,
You make me feel more special than anyone else.
I see you each day,
But will never get bored.
I've tried my hardest, it's now your turn
And that's all that matters to me!

Emily Needham (12)
New Mills School, New Mills

What Matters To Me

W hen my friend is around
H e cheers me up when I'm down
A ll day, every day he makes me laugh
T he day should never end when he is around

M y family care for me
A lways, through thick and thin
T he family abroad
T he family near and far
E very day I enjoy when they're around
R ubbish days, they're not with me
S pecial families are very comforting

T he hamster is my animal
O n the day I got her she was very special

M y sister's rat has bitten her a lot
E very day he draws blood.

Ben Pullan (11)
New Mills School, New Mills

Thunderstorms

T housands of raindrops falling down
H undreds of rumbles in the sky
U nder umbrellas people hurry
N obody wants to be soaking wet through
D eep puddles and the flooded floor
E verybody runs for cover
R andom flashing in my eyes
S treaks of lightning across the sky
T he lightning comes, then the thunder
O verhead the dark, grey clouds
R ed cars have their headlights on
M ost people don't like thunderstorms
S adly, I don't agree with them.

Rebecca Allsop (12)
New Mills School, New Mills

Friends And Family

What matters to me is family and friends,
They're always there, not just for a fling,
Through thick and thin,
Rough and tough.
What matters to me is family and friends,
We scream and squabble,
We glosser and gleam,
We're friends forever, whatever the weather.
What matters to me is family and friends,
We fall out and fight,
We throw paddies all night,
Stomping around, the doors slam,
Family forever, always, whenever!

Natalie Williamson (13)
New Mills School, New Mills

What Matters To Me

My family means the world to me,
We go on holiday and go in the sea,
We all love each other,
Me, my sister, father and mother.

My friends mean the world to me,
Beth, Stacey, Charlie, Angel, Megan, Chloe and Lea,
Paris, Alice, Lydia, Georgia, Rachel, Izzy, Keria and Emily,
We are all like one big family.

Play Mario Kart on the Wii,
Trying to win the race before I watch Glee,
I love playing on the Wii,
My sister and me.

Emily Statham (12)
New Mills School, New Mills

What Matters To Me

W atching TV
H olidays
A ero bars
T oast

M odern Warfare 2
A ll chocolate
T ea
T alking to friends
E ating food
R apid firing
S campi

T hrowing stuff
O wning

M aking cake
E ating cake.

Jack Sanders (12)
New Mills School, New Mills

What Matters To Me

I have lots of friends who matter to me,
One of them is small and smart, the other is tall and cool.
They are always there for me, through thick and thin.
They will always be there for me.

My family are special to me,
They are there whenever I am sad or glad.
My mum makes delicious dinners,
My dad is extremely useless.
My brother and sister, I swear, were a curse
And my dog is always there, under my feet.

I care about my bike, I really do,
Whenever I am mad I jump on and pedal as fast as I can.

Oliver Nickisson (11)
New Mills School, New Mills

What Matters To Me

W atching Doctor Who all day,
H ugging my mum and family,
A ll things living and moving,
T o the Earth, the sea and the sky.

M e, my friends and family,
A t my house all day,
T alking about Lego,
T alking about TV,
E verything that I like,
R ushing around all day,
S topping for a snack.

T ravelling to Cyprus,
O n a sunny day.

M e and my family, but
E ach time I think about it the most that matters to me, is me!

Daniel Carr (11)
New Mills School, New Mills

What Matters To Me

W aking up to a new day,
H aving friends and family there for me, each and every day,
A lthough sometimes I may feel sad,
T hey're always there to cheer me up.

M aking every day worthwhile,
A lways making the most of everything,
T rying new things,
T ime spent with friends,
E very living thing on the Planet Earth,
R eaching for my hopes and dreams,
S o many things that can make me happy.

T rying my best
O pportunities I can't miss!

M aking people smile,
E verything matters to me!

Frances Cope (12)
New Mills School, New Mills

What Matters To Me

W hat matters to me
H ighrise is my favourite map
A t home is my safest place
T wo of my mates are Jack and Ben

M y nan is the best, she buys me lots of things
A nimals are cute, especially dogs
T he television programmes I watch
T he games I play on my PS3
E van is a cool dude
R eading I like to do
S earch and Destroy is my best game mode

T he place I go on holiday is Cornwall
O n my bed I relax

M usic is a fun thing
E nglish is an extremely hard thing.

Jordan Robinson (12)
New Mills School, New Mills

Call Of Duty

COD 7, Black Ops, nearly out, soon
Comes out in a month, I'm over the moon
Killstreaks and call signs,
Soon they'll be all mine

Look at my Javelin,
So that it's travelling,
Headshot, 360, silent shot,
I do them a lot.

Headshot, long shot, commando pro
When I die I get so low
COD 5, COD 6 are so cool
If you hate it you are a fool!

Evan McCullough (12)
New Mills School, New Mills

94

What Matters To Me

W aking up in the morning
H anging out with my friends
A ll the things we do
T hrowing and kicking balls against the wall

M y dog is the best
A t the fields and at the park
T hrowing the ball
T hrowing the stick
E ither way she likes it
R abbits get chased
S peeding away

T ango orange
O r Coke

M mm, it tastes nice
E ach day I do these things, these matter to me!

Jake Derbyshire (12)
New Mills School, New Mills

Sleeper Creeper

I like to sleep
But then a little creep
Comes to peep
And wakes you up
'Cos it's time for education

When you're a dreamer
You soon become a screamer
'Cos the dream becomes a nightmare
And it makes you hair
Stand on end

But when you wake up
The nightmare starts again
'Cos I have to go to school
Use my brain and act a fool.

Matthew Jones (12)
New Mills School, New Mills

Friends

F riends are fun,
    to trust and to care for you
R espect
    your friends
I have best friends and lots of other friends, they are special,
    they're my best friends in the world
E lla and Summer, I've known forever, they're both close to my heart
    as well as the rest
N icole, I've not known for the longest, but it just shows that you
    don't need to know them for long to be your best friend
D esire
    your friends
S ometimes we fall out but because we're friends we can make up
    every time.

Abby Ward (13)
New Mills School, New Mills

Featured Poets:
DEAD POETS
AKA Mark Grist & MC Mixy

Mark Grist and MC Mixy joined forces to become the 'Dead Poets' in 2008.

Since then Mark and Mixy have been challenging the preconceptions of poetry and hip hop across the country. As 'Dead Poets', they have performed in venues ranging from nightclubs to secondary schools; from festivals to formal dinners. They've appeared on Radio 6 Live with Steve Merchant, they've been on a national tour with Phrased and Confused and debuted their show at the 2010 Edinburgh Fringe, which was a huge success.

Both Mark and Mixy work on solo projects as well as working together as the 'Dead Poets'. Both have been Peterborough's Poet Laureate, with Mixy holding the title for 2010.

The 'Dead Poets' are available for workshops in your school as well as other events. Visit www.deadpoetry.co.uk for further information and to contact the guys!

Read on to pick up some fab writing tips!

Your WORKSHOPS

In these workshops we are going to look at writing styles and examine some literary techniques that the 'Dead Poets' use. Grab a pen, and let's go!

Rhythm Workshop

Rhythm in writing is like the beat in music. Rhythm is when certain words are produced more forcefully than others, and may be held for longer duration. The repetition of a pattern is what produces a 'rhythmic effect'. The word rhythm comes from the Greek meaning of 'measured motion'.

Count the number of syllables in your name. Then count the number of syllables in the following line, which you write in your notepad: 'My horse, my horse, will not eat grass'.

Now, highlight the longer sounding syllables and then the shorter sounding syllables in a different colour.

Di dum, di dum, di dum, di dum is a good way of summing this up.

You should then try to write your own lines that match this rhythm. You have one minute to see how many you can write!

Examples include:
'My cheese smells bad because it's hot'
and
'I do not like to write in rhyme'.

For your poem, why don't you try to play with the rhythm? Use only longer beats or shorter beats? Create your own beat and write your lines to this?

Rhyme Workshop

Start off with the phrase 'I'd rather be silver than gold' in your notepad. and see if you can come up with lines that rhyme with it -

'I'd rather have hair than be bald'
'I'd rather be young than be old'
'I'd rather be hot than cold'
'I'd rather be bought than sold'

Also, pick one of these words and see how many rhymes you can find:

Rose

Wall

Warm

Danger

What kinds of rhymes did you come up with? Are there differences in rhymes? Do some words rhyme more cleanly than others? Which do you prefer and why?

Lists Workshop

Game - you (and you can ask your friends or family too) to write as many reasons as possible for the following topics:

Annoying things about siblings

The worst pets ever

The most disgusting ingredients for a soup you can think of

Why not try writing a poem with the same first 2, 3 or 4 words?

I am ...

Or

I love it when ...

Eg:

I am a brother

I am a listener

I am a collector of secrets

I am a messer of bedrooms.

Onomatopoeia Workshop

Divide a sheet of A4 paper into 8 squares.

You then have thirty seconds to draw/write what could make the following sounds:

Splash	Ping
Drip	Bang
Rip	Croak
Crack	Splash

Now try writing your own ideas of onomatopoeia. Why might a writer include onomatopoeia in their writing?

Repetition Workshop

Come up with a list of words/ phrases, aim for at least 5. You now must include one of these words in your piece at least 6 times. You aren't allowed to place these words/ phrases at the beginning of any of the lines.

Suggested words/phrases:

Why

Freedom

Laughing

That was the best day ever

I can't find the door

I'm in trouble again

The best

Workshop
POETRY 101

Below is a poem written especially for poetry matters, by MC Mixy. Why not try and write some more poems of your own?

What is Matter?

© MC Mixy

What matters to me may not be the same things that matter to you
You may not agree with my opinion mentality or attitude
The order in which I line up my priorities to move
Choose to include my view and do what I do due to my mood
And state of mind
I make the time to place the lines on stacks of paper and binds
Concentrate on my artwork hard I can't just pass and scrape behind
Always keep close mates of mine that make things right
And even those who can't … just cos I love the way they can try
What matters to me is doing things the right way
It's tough this game of life we play what we think might stray from what
others might say
In this world of individuality we all wanna bring originality
Live life and drift through casually but the vicious reality is
Creativity is unique
Opinions will always differ but if you figure you know the truth, speak
So many things matter to me depending on how tragically deep you wanna
go
I know I need to defy gravity on this balance beam
As I laugh and breathe draft and read map the scene practise piece smash
the beat and graphic release
Visual and vocal it's a standard procedure
Have to believe and don't bite the hand when it feeds ya

If you wanna be a leader you need to stay out of the pen where the sheep
are
The things that matter to me are
My art and my friends
That will stay from the start to the end
People will do things you find hard to amend
Expect the attacks and prepare you gotta be smart to defend
I put my whole heart in the blend the mass is halved yet again
I'm marked by my pen a big fish fighting sharks of men
In a small pond
Dodging harpoons and nets hooks and predators tryna dismember ya
I won't let them I won't get disheartened I can fend for myself
As long as I'm doing what's important
I'm my mind where I'm supported is a just cause to be supporting
In these appalling hard times I often find myself falling when
Only two aspects of my life keep me sane and allow me to stand tall again
Out of all of them two is a small number
It's a reminder I remind ya to hold necessity and let luxury fall under
Try to avoid letting depression seep through
Take the lesson we actually need a lot less than we think we do
So what matters to you?
They may be similar to things that matter to me
I'm actually lacking the need of things I feel would help me to succeed
Though I like to keep it simple, I wanna love, I wanna breed
I'm one of many individuals in this world where importance fluctuates and
varies
Things that matter will come and go
But the ones that stay for long enough must be worth keeping close
If you're not sure now don't watch it you'll know when you need to know
Me, I think I know now … yet I feel and fear I don't.

Turn overleaf for a poem by Mark Grist and some fantastic hints and tips!

Workshop
POETRY 101

What Tie Should I Wear Today?

© Mark Grist

I wish I had a tie that was suave and silk and slick,
One with flair, that's debonair and would enchant with just one flick,
Yeah, I'd like that … a tie that's hypnotizing,
I'd be very restrained and avoid womanising,
But all the lady teachers would still say 'Mr Grist your tie's so charming!'
As I cruise into their classrooms with it striking and disarming.
At parents' evenings my tie's charm would suffice,
In getting mums to whisper as they leave 'Your English teacher seems nice!'

Or maybe an evil-looking tie - one that's the business,
Where students will go 'Watch out! Mr Grist is
on the prowl with that evil tie.'
The one that cornered Josh and then ripped out his eye.
Yeah no one ever whispers, no one ever sniggers,
Or my tie would rear up and you'd wet your knickers.
Maybe one girl just hasn't heard the warning,
Cos she overslept and turned up late to school that morning,
And so I'd catch her in my lesson yawning … oh dear.
I'd try to calm it down, but this tie's got bad ideas.
It'd size the girl up and then just as she fears,
Dive in like a serpent snapping at her ears.
There'd be a scream, some blood and lots and lots of tears,
And she wouldn't be able to yawn again for years.

Or maybe … a tie that everyone agrees is mighty fine
And people travel from miles around to gawp at the design
I'd like that … a tie that pushes the boundaries of tieware right up to the limit
It'd make emos wipe their tears away while chavs say 'It's wicked innit?'
and footy lads would stop me with 'I'd wear that if I ever won the cup.'
And I'd walk through Peterborough to slapped backs, high fives, thumbs up
While monosyllabic teenagers would just stand there going 'Yup.'

I don't know. I'd never be sure which of the three to try
As any decision between them would always end a tie.

Tips and Advice for
PERFORMING
Your Poem

So you've written your poem, now how about performing it.
Whether you read your poem for the first time in front of your class, school
or strangers at an open mic event or poetry slam, these tips will help you
make the best of your performance.

Breathe and try to relax.

**Every poet that reads in front of people for the first time feels a bit nervous,
when you're there you are in charge and nothing serious can go wrong.**

People at poetry slams or readings are there to support the poets. They really are!

If you can learn your poem off by heart that is brilliant, however having a piece of paper or notebook with your work in is fine, though try not to hide behind these.

**It's better to get some eye contact with the audience.
If you're nervous find a friendly face to focus on.**

Try to read slowly and clearly and enjoy your time in the spotlight.

Don't rush up to the microphone, make sure it's at the right height for you and if you need it adjusted ask one of the team around you.

**Before you start, stand up as straight as you can and get your body as
comfortable as you can and remember to hold your head up.**

The microphone can only amplify what what's spoken into it; if you're very loud you might
end up deafening people and if you only whisper or stand too far away you won't be heard.

When you say something before your poem, whether that's hello or just the title of your poem, try and have a listen to how loud you sound. If you're too quiet move closer to the microphone, if you're too loud move back a bit.

**Remember to breathe! Don't try to say your poem so quickly you can't find
time to catch your breath.**

And finally, **enjoy!**

Poetry FACTS

Here are a selection of fascinating poetry facts!

No word in the English language rhymes with 'MONTH'.

William Shakespeare was born on 23rd April 1564 and died on 23rd April 1616.

The haiku is one of the shortest forms of poetic writing.
Originating in Japan, a haiku poem is only seventeen syllables, typically broken down into three lines of five, seven and five syllables respectively.

The motto of the Globe Theatre was 'totus mundus agit histrionem' (the whole world is a playhouse).

The Children's Laureate award was an idea by Ted Hughes and Michael Morpurgo.

The 25th January each year is Burns' Night, an occasion in honour of Scotland's national poet Robert Burns.

Spike Milligan's 'On the Ning Nang Nong' was voted the UK's favourite comic poem in 1998.

Did you know *onomatopoeia* means the word you use sounds like the word you are describing – like the rain *pitter-patters* or the snow *crunches* under my foot.

'Go' is the shortest complete sentence in the English language.

Did you know rhymes were used in olden days to help people remember the news? Ring-o'-roses is about the Plague!

The Nursery Rhyme 'Old King Cole' is based on a real king and a real historical event. King Cole is supposed to have been an actual monarch of Britain who ruled around 200 A.D.

Edward Lear popularised the limerick with his poem 'The Owl and the Pussy-Cat'.

Lewis Carroll's poem 'The Jabberwocky' is written in nonsense style.

POEM – noun

1. a composition in verse, esp. one that is characterized by a highly developed artistic form and by the use of heightened language and rhythm to express an intensely imaginative interpretation of the subject.

Poetry TIPS

We have compiled some helpful tips for you budding poets...

In order to write poetry, read lots of poetry!

Keep a notebook with you at all times so you can write whenever (and wherever) inspiration strikes.

Every line of a poem should be important to the poem and interesting to read. A poem with only 3 great lines should be 3 lines long.

Use an online rhyming dictionary to improve your vocabulary.

Use free workshops and help sheets to learn new poetry styles.

Experiment with visual patterns - does your written poetry create a good pattern on the page?

Try to create pictures in the reader's mind - aim to fire the imagination.

Develop your voice. Become comfortable with how you write.

Listen to criticism, and try to learn from it, but don't live or die by it.

Say what you want to say, let the reader decide what it means.

Notice what makes other's poetry memorable. Capture it, mix it up and make it your own. (Don't copy other's work word for word!)

Go wild. Be funny. Be serious. Be whatever you want!

Grab hold of something you feel - anything you feel - and write it.

The more you write, the more you develop. Write poetry often.

Use your imagination, your own way of seeing.

Feel free to write a bad poem, it will develop your 'voice'.

Did you know ...?

'The Epic of Gilgamesh' was written thousands of years ago in Mesopotamia and is the oldest poem on record.

The *premier* magazine
for creative young people
Wordsmith

A platform for your imagination and creativity. Showcase your ideas and have your say. Welcome to a place where like-minded young people express their personalities and individuality knows no limits.

For further information visit ***www.youngwriters.co.uk***.

A peek into Wordsmith world ...

Poetry and Short Stories

We feature both themed and non-themed work every issue. Previous themes have included; dreams and aspirations, superhero stories and ghostly tales.

Next Generation Author

This section devotes two whole pages to one of our readers' work. The perfect place to showcase a selection of your poems, stories or both!

Guest Author Features & Workshops

Interesting and informative tutorials on different styles of poetry and creative writing. Famous authors and illustrators share their advice with us on how to create gripping stories and magical picturebooks. Novelists like Michael Morpurgo and Celia Rees go under the spotlight to answer our questions.

The fun doesn't stop there ...

Every issue we tell you what events are coming up across the country. We keep you up to date with the latest film and book releases and we feature some yummy recipes to help feed the brain and get the creative juices flowing.

So with all this and more, Wordsmith is *the* magazine to be reading.

If you are too young for Wordsmith magazine or have a younger friend who enjoys creative writing, then check out Scribbler!. Scribbler! is for 7-11 year-olds and is jam-packed full of brilliant features, young writers' work, competitions and interviews too. For further information check out ***www.youngwriters.co.uk*** or ask an adult to call us on (01733) 890066.

To get an adult to subscribe to either magazine for you, ask them to visit the website or give us a call.

My Dog

My big dog
My dog's big
And eats everything
Off its plate

My dog's big
And he is my best mate

My dog's big
And he likes his walks
My dog's big
I'm sure he can talk

My dog's big
And loves his treat
My dog's big
But shh, he's asleep!

Luke Bradley (11)
New Mills School, New Mills

What Matters

What matters is
The Earth
The sky
The wood
The hill
The mountain
Every bird, the speck so high
The rabbit in the valley
My family, the way they sigh
To show they really care
And friends, people always near
In your mind, if not in person
But just because pets, with breath of fear
Run away, doesn't mean they don't matter.

Ellen Scottney (13)
New Mills School, New Mills

Autumn

Autumn brings summer to her knees,
Wind, wind, whizzing past trees,
As dead leaves fall,
Fall to the ground.

Autumn turns everything green to yellow, to brown . . .
Everything changing now,
For winter to come.

Autumn, most of the animals sleep,
Waiting for summer to return,
Leaves on the ground,
Spread about,
Every inch covered by a grey, gloomy sky.

Autumn passes,
Winter too,
Soon everything will be renewed.

Melissa Clinton (11)
New Mills School, New Mills

Seize The Day

You can't wait forever,
Because you'll grow old,
You don't have a stone heart -
But a heart of gold.

You don't know it yet,
But you can change the future,
You shine like the sun
And are as stunning as nature.

Please join me now,
Before it's too late,
Time flies by, now
Find your soulmate.

So do it now,
Take a chance,
Or live forever
Without romance.

Lois Ford (14)
Newport Girls' High School, Newport

My Dream

I close my eyes, I fade away,
I drift at my own pace,
I am going there again,
I am going to my place.

My place is filled with happiness,
My place can be quite sad,
My place is many different things,
Sometimes it makes me mad.

Sometimes there are oceans
And others there are sky,
But one thing I can count on,
I'll never want to say goodbye.

If I want I can see my friends
And even camels too,
Once I saw a hot air balloon,
Every night there is something new.

But, often, when I'm in my place,
Similar things happen in the day,
But they are normally a bit better
And I prefer it that way.

So when the enemy comes
And discovers my worst fear,
I know that I am safe,
He will slowly disappear.

Because, however hard I wish,
However hard I try,
I know my place isn't real,
Only to me, myself and I.

Everyone has a place,
A place of thought and fear and shame,
But I think mine is extra special,
I'm sure everyone feels the same.

And when it's time to wake,
When it's time to go,
I remember I'll be back again soon,

110

I'll be there tonight I know.

I pop in sometimes to say hello,
When I get tired of it being the day,
But it never normally lasts for long,
Everyone else gets in the way.

So I prefer my adventures,
The ones that happen at night,
When the moon is watching over me,
When the stars are shining bright.

And sometimes I dream,
Dream of all sorts of things
And sometimes they come true,
But mostly they never do.

Lucy Young (12)
Newport Girls' High School, Newport

Winter Walk

Cold, white flakes land on the hills,
As I stroll forward into the night,
I am alone in this desolate landscape, all is silent,
the snowfall is ongoing.
My footfalls land with a crunch upon the crystal ice,
My breath billows out in a cloud,
As I pull my woolly bobble hat over my ears,
The sun is sinking over the horizon, like dripping blood.
As I trek into the distance,
The ground is becoming covered in a blanket of white,
Frozen tears fall from the clouds,
As I repetitively put one foot in front of the other.
I listen to the silence, the sound of nothing.
I am tiring,
The cold is seeping into my muscles,
The wind bites my cheeks,
I am Nature's version of a frozen ghost town.
Trees are covered in a gift from the skies,
My boots now sink into whiteness with a satisfying squeak.
Streetlights glow above me, but flicker in my vision
As fluffy clumps tumble frantically down.
I breathe a sigh of relief when I see a window,
Inside children play and marvel at the snow then spot me,
I have arrived.

Tasleem Branton (11)
Newport Girls' High School, Newport

Everything Tells A Story

A chess board,
Just two simple colours,
An optical illusion,
Playing tricks on your mind.

A wall full of bricks,
So many different shades,
Of browns and blues,
With reds and maroons.

The deep blue sea,
The ripples on the surface,
The stillness underneath
And the animals so beautiful.

The clouds in the sky,
Like candyfloss,
Or cotton wool,
Floating all alone.

The miracles in front of us,
That we never even notice,
The way that everything tells a story
And a beautiful one, at that.

Bryony Green (11)
Newport Girls' High School, Newport

Master Of The Sky

He searches the sky, watching for prey,
Watching and waiting, night and day.
His eyes as sharp as a needle's point,
He spreads his wings and prepares to fly,
He is the master of the sky.

He chases food, large and small,
Perching on trees, short and tall,
Nothing can escape his deadly grip,
No prey should even try,
He is the master of the sky.

He moves with tremendous grace
And twists and turns at amazing pace,
His speed only few can match,
The air takes his movements high,
He is the master of the sky.

He gives his partner many supplies,
So that every chick of his survives.
He is the hunter and so is she,
He makes all the animals cry,
He is the master of the sky.

He is a bird with strength so great
And he kills at a very high rate,
His talons are like small spikes,
When he squawks I hear his sigh,
He is the master of the sky.

His feathers give a golden glow
And on them the wind does blow,
He is, to me, like a treasure,
When he cries I wonder why,
He is the master of the sky.

His beak is like a razor blade,
Many meals it has made,
Animals fear his entire being,
Numerous homes does he spy,
He is the master of the sky.

His body is of great build,

When I see him I am thrilled,
He is a magnificent bird,
This golden eagle's time is nigh,
He is the master of the sky.

Emma Owen [12]
Newport Girls' High School, Newport

The Valley

As I stand on the top of the huge green hill,
The springy strands of grass sway around me,
To music only they can hear.
A soft breeze wafts over me,
Bringing with it the divine aroma of wild flowers.
The bright, galleon gold sun smiles down,
Her fingers of soft, delicate light tickling my face,
Whilst the candyfloss clouds balance in the sky above me,
Dreamily floating past.

I look down upon the scene below me,
Breathing in the fresh, heavenly air.
A blanket of rainforest stretches as far as the eye can see,
As dense as the thickest undergrowth.
The sea of green is a patchwork cover,
Lime green, deep green, the darkest green known and many more.
Only a blue stream penetrates its luscious darkness,
The green waves giving way to show it feeding into a river,
As clear as a crystal.

The rolls of landscape happily bathe in the sun,
Laughing at each other,
But in a friendly way.
A blue jay soars across the sky,
Almost camouflaged but for his beautiful singing voice calling out.

But wait, loud men's voices,
Resounding in the pretty valley.
The roar of machines seems to strangle me,
Bursting my ears;
Trees are falling all around me.
I am afraid.
The smell of smoke, flames licking at me
And I am screaming in anguish
And torture,
Screaming,
Screaming, death.

Elizabeth Haigh (11)
Newport Girls' High School, Newport

Nature's Terms

The new year begins with the season we call winter,
A time where all the money goes to the vintner,
Just because it's Christmas time,
Everybody loves a bit of red wine.

It's a time when the snow falls a metre thick on the ground
And made into snowballs that are always thrown around,
Sitting by the nice, warm fire is where I like to be,
Whilst Santa is coming along dropping presents off to me.

Next comes spring, new baby animals are born,
It's the time of the year where it begins to get warm,
Everything awakens, things become green,
At this time of year it's a beautiful scene.

Now comes the summer, the time I adore,
It is much, much warmer than it was before,
A time for holidays, fun times abroad,
It's a time of year we should all applaud.

A time for ice cream in the pool
Where you can have time just to cool,
In the hot summer sun is where I like to be,
Before autumn arrives, catching up with me.

Here comes fall,
The most attractive time of all,
The trees turn amber, the grass begins to go brown,
All of a sudden the leaves all fall down.

It's the time of year we can all enjoy,
Before it all turns cold and begins to annoy,
It's the last season of the year
When the end begins to appear.

After fall we come back to wintertime,
So let's go back to the beginning of this rhyme.

Laura Jones (11)
Newport Girls' High School, Newport

Selfishness

Elegant ballgowns move across the floor
As well-dressed guests sweep through the doors
Fine new suits fill my mind
With hand-made dresses of every kind

Grand old memories from so long ago
Remind me of the times I used to know
Money galore is how my life used to be
But this is no longer the life that I lead

Now I spend my days alone on the street
Wandering around aimlessly
Because I never cared for anyone else
I live each long second all by myself

If only I knew what it's like
To have no home to go to at night
Then maybe I would have been less mean
To the people I hurt, because now I see

That everyone's equal and there's no one to hate
But I guess that thought's a little too late
Because what good does it do to knock others back
When you'll only end up worse off than that

I should have seen then all the pain I did cause
When I left others lying both shattered and torn
All the pain they went through, I know what it's like
When I brushed them aside, when I ruined each life

Because I was selfish, because I couldn't care less
Because I thought nothing mattered but myself
I have lost everything, all I did own
Including my dignity, now I walk alone.

Eleanor Wolz (11)
Newport Girls' High School, Newport

I Like That Stuff

My mum thinks it's disgusting,
I drink it till my stomach's busting,
Dr Pepper, I like that stuff.

LG Pink Taco Lite,
Ring and text all night,
Phones, I like that stuff.

The Simpsons and design shows,
Really, anything goes,
TV, I like that stuff.

Yellow, orange, red and pink,
I really, really love their stink,
Roses, I like that stuff.

Marvin, Ortise, JB and Aston,
I am their number one fan,
JLS, I like that stuff.

Wake up, all refreshed,
It simply is the best,
Sleep, I like that stuff.

Filled with nutty cream,
It's my ideal dream,
Bueno, I like that stuff.

Swim and sit in the sun,
Licking ice cream, it's so fun,
Holidays, I like that stuff.

Does all the Hoovering,
Really thinks she can sing,
My mum, I love that stuff.

Megan Curran (11)
Newport Girls' High School, Newport

This Feeling Is Bad

There's somebody I miss,
I miss them so much,
But I went too far,
I'm such
An idiot,
This can't be a guy,
This person to me
Was my only best friend.

I feel so ashamed,
I lost all their trust,
I miss being always
Annoyingly fussed,
All of the time
I did what she said,
Until one day
I ran and fled.

I don't know why I did it,
I was out of my mind,
It took me some time,
To realise my kind,
My kind was a beast,
Building up their hate,
Until they wanted
No more to wait.

I don't like the feeling,
That I have in my heart,
Oh will this sadness
Ever depart?

Charlotte Coles (11)
Newport Girls' High School, Newport

All I Have Left

All I have left
Are the memories
The ones I have
Cannot be shared
Cannot be erased
Cannot be changed

The ones from the heart
The brain
The soul
Each one unique
Individual
And memorable

Arguments
Making up
The best, the worst
And of course, the unstoppable

All of them;
Memories
Regrets
Secrets
And unsettled stories

Because of your disappearance.

Rachael Holmes (12)
Newport Girls' High School, Newport

The Girl On The Bouncy Hopper

There once was a girl from Peru
Who thought she could bounce to the moon
So she jumped on her hopper
And no one could stop her
Except for a smelly baboon!

Natalie Webb (11)
Newport Girls' High School, Newport

Four Seasons

Start of the new school year
Browns and reds emerge, green vanishes
The swaying trees reject the turning laves
The crumbling, skeletal brown leaves suffocate the bare ground
The days grow shorter

Your breath has a life of its own
as ice hugs the dull red walls
The pond is a multi-tasker, as it is a mirror
and a personal ice rink
The naked trees can only stand there
as a blizzard storms by
Snow controls the Earth

A million flowers spring up, as though they've been having a nap
The trees start reclothing
The rain is beautiful as it continuously pounds the world
The sky is filled with cotton clouds
The sun starts to show

It's fun in the sun
The beach cunningly lures people in all day
The sun gently and gracefully strokes my face
One warm, summer morning
It's the end of the school year.

Katie Pauling (11)
Newport Girls' High School, Newport

Home

H appy homes are wonderful places
O n which a sturdy, sheltering roof sits
M agical feelings swim inside
E rasing all fears from your mind.

Heather Todd (11)
Newport Girls' High School, Newport

A Rosebud Blooms

A rosebud blooms as day goes by
And the petals begin to fade,
As day moves into the night,
It's on the floor they lay.

A rosebud blooms as day goes by,
So you should seize the day,
Don't put off to tomorrow
What you can do today.

A rosebud blooms as day goes by
And petals begin to fall.
So seize the day before they fade
And take today as well.

A rosebud blooms as day goes by
And the petals they will fade,
As day moves into the night
They will lie there in the shade.

Flo Burton (13)
Newport Girls' High School, Newport

A Single Thing

A single flame was all I needed to show my love for you,
A single rose was all I needed to show that we weren't through,
A single pearl was all I needed for our love to be true,
A single love note was all I needed for our love to renew.

A single dance was all I needed to show that we were never still,
A single pin was all I needed for our love to never kill,
A single hug was all I needed when I was ill,
A single thing, a single thing, always will.

Maisie McCormick (11)
Newport Girls' High School, Newport

Or Voyage Alone

Time shows no mercy,
It never seems to sleep.
It can gently blow past you
Or pass in a giant leap.

Life is like a deep, dark ocean,
Once you're on let it sway,
Grab the chance before it's too late,
Don't hide yourself away.

Suddenly, it's there, in your grasp,
But shortly it turns, like a lightning flash,
There is no choice but to let it go
And watch it burn, turn into ash.

The world is like a bottomless pit,
Once you have gone you can never come back,
When you are left to live life on your own,
You can easily slip off track.

Once you've let go, it's too late,
All strength has been blown,
No contact, it must be fate,
For you it's a voyage alone.

Kirsten Sinclair (14)
Newport Girls' High School, Newport

What I Never Did . . .

Telling a story I will never forget,
One bursting with great regret,
Full of love and desire,
Even after I retire.

To celebrate the life of my treasured one,
Who was a whole load of fun -
I missed her soul when she had done,
Passed away, her love gone.

I miss her dearly, she was my idol,
Yet she made me so very bridle,
When she never listened to what they said
And therefore passed away to the dead.

To celebrate the life of my treasured one,
Who was a whole load of fun -
I missed her soul when she had done,
Passed away, her love gone.

She was an undiscovered star to me,
Being everything she could be,
But I never said I love you,
And now there's nothing I can do.

Emma Scriven (13)
Newport Girls' High School, Newport

Carpe Diem

I am old
And withered I may be
But I used all my time
That was left for me

When I was young
And when times came
I took a chance
And played the game

The game of life -
How fun it could be
But time was catching up -
With me

I saw it swiftly run
While I turned grey
It reminded me of joy and laughter
Which made me what I am today

I am today what the years have made me
Life is merely but an equation! A sum!
Two words made my mind up
Carpe diem! Carpe diem!

Shama Nataraja (13)
Newport Girls' High School, Newport

Fly Away

When those downing, rainy days come around,
The happiness inside you must be found,
So that you make the most of every day
And your negative thoughts are blown away.

Life's not just money, items and toys,
It's happiness, love and a thousand joys.
But there's always a worry, a thought, a sigh
And something to stop you ending on a high.

So when those opportunities catch your eye,
Do not hesitate, give it a try.
Every time the wind blows, time is moving on . . .
So taking at least one chance is better than none.

To leave it this late is bad enough,
But waiting any longer will be even more tough.
So get ready to seize the day,
Take your chances and fly away.

Emily Fowler (13)
Newport Girls' High School, Newport

Live And Learn To Love Each Day

Life is long but the days are short
Live each moment as your last
Keep looking forward, don't look back
Don't swell upon your past.

The grains of time slip through your fingers
Before you know - they're gone
It's all about the taking part
Not if you've lost or won.

Take a chance on life sometimes
Don't pour it down the drain
Chase you dreams while you still can
Chances won't come round again.

As hot as the sun
Dreams sizzle away
So live and learn
To love each day.

Tanisha Hanna-Beards (14)
Newport Girls' High School, Newport

The Butterfly

Youth is like a butterfly
If you wait too long
It will flutter by
Just as the words to a song
Drift away up to the sky

Your beauty does not compare
With she that does fly
Through the air
You are the gentle butterfly

So don't be shy
You are the beautiful butterfly.

Alice Simons (14)
Newport Girls' High School, Newport

128

Fan

Pack your camera, pen and book,
Waste no time, just go and look,
When those who always steal the scene
Are liberated from the screen.

Harsh the journey you will make,
Devoured by a queuing snake,
A chance to see, a change to touch,
That icon whom you worship so much.

So if you want the flesh made real,
Tell them now how they make you feel,
Brave the weather and the crowd;
Grab their attention, shout out loud!

Your idol's looks aren't made to last,
Beyond the role for which they're cast,
When they are old and you are tired,
You'll never meet who you admired.

Serena Gough (13)
Newport Girls' High School, Newport

Skeletal Hands

Skeletal hands from trees that sway,
Waiting to come alive, waiting for that day.

Skeletal hands that grab you in the dark,
Not saying a word, not leaving a mark.

Skeletal hands that crunch you up,
Small as a mouse, smaller than a cup.

The skeletal hands are crooked and long,
Gently singing their attack song.

When the howling winds turn to a purr,
The skeletal hands are one to stir . . .

Amber Bickerton (11)
Newport Girls' High School, Newport

The Sand Timer

As you sit at home dreaming
The hourglass does not cease to turn
Each moment lost, is gone forever
Time cannot be undone

In an unburdened youth
It is difficult to understand
Chances gradually trickle away
As responsibility climbs

Grasp happiness whilst it is in the light
Darkness smothers hope
Chances will slowly pour into
The bottomless pit of regret

Squeeze the life from each grain
Rejoice the chances you have
As the light will surely fade
And time will run out.

Rachel Bromley (14)
Newport Girls' High School, Newport

The Cage

You worked so hard
For the job of a lifetime.
Leaving the country
Was your only lifeline.

But the decision you made -
To stick with your dearest,
Was a decision to regret -
Now boredom is nearest.

Stuck in your comfort zone,
There is no way out.
Like a bear trapped in a cage,
Like a fish in a drought.

You cannot take back
The choices you have made,
But you can think positive -
Till the end of your days.

Alex Jones (13)
Newport Girls' High School, Newport

Home

Home to me is Canada, with all its tall trees,
Not England, with all the teas.

Canada has the mountains,
England has the fountains.

Canada has the moose,
England has the goose.

Canada has the beavers,
England invented all the levers.

Canada has the wheat mills,
England has the rolling hills.

Canada has the saltwater hose,
England has the Tudor rose.

Canada is where my family resides,
England is where the rest of us hide.

Elizabeth Bearblock (11)
Newport Girls' High School, Newport

Lost Souls

All those dreams they didn't fulfil,
All those years they could not live,
People die and people kill,
Someone help me to forgive.

Lives are lost and blood is spilt,
Lost souls are forsaken,
First comes death, then comes guilt,
All memories are taken.

So much pain and so much death,
Lost souls are forsaken,
So just remember every breath,
That you have ever taken.

Lois Payne (11)
Newport Girls' High School, Newport

Windmill

There it stands, bold,
With large elegant arms
Which spin round and round gracefully.
Its welcoming sound of wind hurling around drifts swiftly,
As it peacefully gathers eyes.
Daringly, children approach it as the turbines deafen the land.
Cars travel past without a glance, but with a stare.
The world timidly holds the body safe and sturdy to the ground.
The fan turns faster and faster with the power of the wind.
Its fans are the size of giants' feet
When you near the rapid fans,
It's like the whole world is an enormous tornado,
As it makes others tremble in their seats.
It slowly enjoys standing there amongst its friends,
The ground trembles, fighting the fierce, roaring lion underneath.
How can such a large thing save the generations to come?

Jameela Sheikh (11)
Newport Girls' High School, Newport

Racism

In a tiny corner there,
Prejudice is born,
It grows around the world and back,
Till the light of dawn.

Why do we live like pieces in chess,
So we are all apart?
It goes from joy in our happy hearts
To trails from our hearts.

It's all around on Planet Earth
It makes everyone cry, boo hoo,
So stop this nonsense and all make friends,
But would this happen to you?

Lucy Gibbs (11)
Newport Girls' High School, Newport

The Wolf

The wolf's eyes are like rubies sparkling in the sunlight,
They're demon eyes,
The wolf's nose is like a commanding officer,
Telling everyone where to go next,
It's a demon's nose.
The wolf's legs carry him everywhere, making the wolf depend on them,
They need to work together desperately,
They're what carries the demon!

The wolf's teeth are like daggers, freshly sharpened, ready for use,
They were made for a demon's kill.
The wolf's ears are spiked up, they work all hours of the day,
All days a week, never ever stopping to rest,
They're demon's ears.
The wolf's tail is so cute and cuddly, fluffy and cool,
It's not all evil!

Francesca Storey (11)
Newport Girls' High School, Newport

Halloween At My House

What is it about this spooky date
That makes everybody quiver and shake?
My house looks creepy, dark and cold,
Or is it just because it's old?
Did something move in the shadows there?
A sudden shiver, who touched my hair?
My palms sweat, my heart pounds,
What is that creaking sound?
I hear groans as I reach the stairs,
Should I go up?
Would I dare?
Everything looks scary in the dark at night,
Yet it all disappears as the morning breaks light . . .
Phew!

Orla Pascall (11)
Newport Girls' High School, Newport

Senses

Sweet as chocolate,
Smell like a rose,
Strong as a wrestler,
A few of the pros!

If only I'd come to my senses,
Time to put up my defences.

Sour as a lemon,
Scary like Halloween,
Slow as a wet weekend,
Soft like gelatine.

I've come to my senses now,
But it's taken a long time,
Now it will never happen,
We have both lost our prime.

Katy Richards (13)
Newport Girls' High School, Newport

Autumn

The leaves crunching,
Animals munching.

Horses in the field,
Looking at the farmer's yield.

Cold days drawing in,
Winter is soon to begin.

Scarves, hats, gloves too,
My brother's looking forward to throwing a snowball or two.

Frosty mornings start to begin,
When the colder nights draw in.

Numb fingers, toes too,
I've got my thermals and so should you.

Harriet Pope (11)
Newport Girls' High School, Newport

A Beautiful Place

A beautiful place that captures my sight
And sparkles like magic, like dynamite

A comfortable place that's safe and warm
A place to curl up and hide from the storm

A sweet-smelling place that pleases my nose
From exotic spices to a delicate rose

A happy place where the sound of
Laughter will shatter glass forever

A mouth-watering place, full of fabulous meals
Oriental spices send me head over heels

A beautiful place, more stunning than Rome
Blissful and friendly, there's no place like home.

Isobel Simons (11)
Newport Girls' High School, Newport

My Future

I wish to blossom
I want to ride the waves
Currents will take me there
And leave behind my wake

Creating prosperity along the way
My heart will find treasure
A treasure to keep

I wish to create a future
I wish my future prosperous
And for it to flower
Like a blood-red rose.

Sean Russell (14)
Nicholas Chamberlaine Technology College, Bedworth

A Child - The World Of Suffering

Children who suffer,
Morning comes and evening falls,
The unfortunate child waits in vain,
For who will help in this situation?

Education could help,
But it could be for the fortunate and wealthy.
What can I do? God has the answer.
An option for some,
Could I go to the street
Where I can get something to eat
Or meet my problems?

Children who suffer,
A day comes and evening comes,
So it falls,
Showers of grief that pour onto my heart.
The rebel comes and seems to have given you a way,
To kill and abduct others is the motion of the day
To an unfortunate child.

God helped and it stopped.
Long as it is, I will suffer more.
Next, I have to struggle
To get my basics in the market.
I walk, sneaking for the ladies' bags
To get a penny for the day.
What could a penny do?

Please answer me, you children who suffer.
What do you think is next?
I escape narrowly from the jaws of death.
I am pulled out
By somebody who could be a friend.
Police! To jail!
I board the car with a siren.

God help me.
Life moves on.
To the rubbish pits I wander,
Looking for something to eat,
Only to find more danger.
A snake bite!
What next . . .

Francis Xavier Ssuna (14)
Nicholas Chamberlaine Technology College, Bedworth

From A Young Age

From a young age
Dance was a passion,
Hearing the music flow into your body
As your feet start to sweep across the floor,
Like you are gliding across a glimmering glistening ice rink,
That's when I found out it was that I need.

From a young age
Dance was a passion,
The sound of tap shoes,
Calmly but loudly pressing to the floor,
Each time you compress your feet a new sound can be heard,
As it sets a noise of a miracle being awoken.

From a young age
Dance was a passion,
The feel of a pair of pink ballet shoes lightly on your feet,
When you spread your feet across,
Brushing sounds are made as feet move to the beat.

From a young age
Dance was a passion,
Leaping and swaying on the cold, wooden floor,
You can't always do it right,
But one thing I have learnt is
If dance was easy it would be football.

Chloe Routley (13)
Nicholas Chamberlaine Technology College, Bedworth

Mothers

They do everything for you
And they do it with love
Their gentle, soft touch
Mothers.

Cooking and cleaning
They do all this and more
Stopping you and brother from creating a war
Mothers.

When times are tough
They're always there
Making you feel safe
Mothers.

Your childhood memories soon disappear
And growing up you soon will think
Soon; it will be me.

They get older
But their love never stops growing
Finally it's your turn
Mothers.

When they're gone you get stronger
Memories flash back
Never forgetting special moments
Mothers.

Chloe Brooks (13)
Nicholas Chamberlaine Technology College, Bedworth

The Moon And The Sun

I see the moon,
Shining so bright,
High up in the sky,
But looks so big.

I can see the face,
Right there, in the moon,
Look! Look! And you will see,
Gazing right at me!

The sky is so black,
Out shines the moon
And purple the sky becomes.

Where is the sun?
I can't see it, must be there somewhere,
All I see is clouds,
The sun hasn't got out of bed yet!

Oh look, over there,
I see you now,
So warm and welcoming,
Hello Sun!

There is no face,
I can't look right at you,
Mum tells me it's bad.

I see how you light up the world,
I see you make the world come alive.

When you come out,
Everyone is too,
How do you do that?

The moon has the stars
They're his friends,
The sun has people
They're her friends.

There is a time when the sun and moon meet,
It's called dusk,
The most beautiful time of day.

We are never alone,
Being watched, but
Make the watchers your friends,
That's what matters to me!

Rea MacCallum (13)
Nicholas Chamberlaine Technology College, Bedworth

Football

Football is my life!
Without it I wouldn't
Have the will to live
Anymore.

But every time I play this
Game the weather battles
With me, trying to force me
To give up. But I go on
And fight the snow
And rain and whatever else it has
To throw at me.

Sometimes I play with my dad
And when I do I don't
Follow the ball; I follow
His shadow.

And when I score a
Goal, my blood shoots
Around my body, then I
Howl in happiness for
My success. My heart
Bounces against my chest
As the ball bounces against
The goalie's net.

Anton Haywood (13)
Nicholas Chamberlaine Technology College, Bedworth

My Childhood

1st of January 1997
That's when my mum had me,
9:33pm; a beautiful baby girl
Was brought into the world.

She's always said that,
Ever since that day,
Since when I've had many birthdays
And still so many to come.

Life's been hard sometimes,
But hey, no one said it was easy.
My little brother was born a year after me
And I'm proud to say he's here with me.

My mom and dad divorced when I was five
And just two years after
My big sister had my niece,
Who is the apple of my eye.

When I was ten, two things happened,
My mum met my stepdad
And my sister had my nephew, my boy,
I love him with all my heart.

Megan Brindley (13)
Nicholas Chamberlaine Technology College, Bedworth

What Really Matters

This is what matters to me
My friends, my family
To look out for them
To be there for them
Then to be there for me
To protect them, no matter what
Them to protect me
My family has always been there for me
I will be there for them
My friends have never let me down
I will not let them down
I need them and they need me
My mum, my dad, my bros, my pets and my mates
They are everything to me
Sometimes I need them
Sometimes they need me
But they're always there and I'm always here
This is all I need in my life
I think this all anyone needs
As long as you're together, it will be alright.

Josh McLoughlin (13)
Nicholas Chamberlaine Technology College, Bedworth

The One I Look Up To . . .

There is a person in my life,
Very similar to me,
I look up to them, they are my idol
And they always will be.

My sister is perfect,
They say nobody's perfect but I have to disagree,
Because every time I look at her
I see a part of me.

She's done everything for me,
Picked my name and bought me things,
Some people dislike their siblings,
But she brings me no shame.

I don't know what profession I will take
When I am older,
I just know that she's all I want to be.

Lucy Jade Barratt (13)
Nicholas Chamberlaine Technology College, Bedworth

Cheating In Sport

Cheating in sport is getting very bad
What matters to me it's getting sad
From footballers diving to win a pen
To match fixing cricket again and again
There are steroids to enhance athletic ability
To drugs that abnormalise a gymnast's agility.

Why do our heroes become such a mess?
Maybe to help relieve the stress
What these people need to realise is that
You will have good days and bad
And as I say, it's getting sad.

Daniel Casey (13)
Nicholas Chamberlaine Technology College, Bedworth

Crunchy Leaves

Crunchy leaves
They fall off the trees
Crunchy leaves
Are good for jumping in

Crunchy leaves
Go crunch under my wheels
Crunchy leaves
Brown, orange, yellow and red

Crunchy leaves
It's cold, wet and windy out there
Crunchy leaves
I like to lie on the carpet in front of the fire to keep warm
Crunchy leaves

It's too cold for me
Crunchy leaves.

Uroosa Iqbal, Connor Coates, Porsha Foster & Aishah
Oak Field School & Sports College, Nottingham

Autumn

I like leaves falling down, falling down,
Red conkers, prickly conkers.

Weather for Wellington boots on cold feet,
Freezing October!

I like Halloween,
Masks and apple bobbing,
Weather for golden syrup on pancakes,
Apple and pumpkin - fantastic!

Scary scarecrows.

Ali Iqbal, William Ferns & Keenan Stewart
Oak Field School & Sports College, Nottingham

Holidays

Holidays are fun days
And lots of sunny days too.

Holidays are for suncream
And lots of delicious ice cream.

Holidays are swimming pools
To jump in and feel cool.

Holidays are golden sands
Which is too hot on which to stand.

Holidays are burning sun
And finally, holidays are fun!

Jade Alana Sykes (12)
Skegness Academy, Skegness

Home

Home is comfy,
Home is safe,
Just like our year base.
People kind,
People not,
Doesn't matter quite that much.
Sausage and mash,
Veg and meat,
All of us together to eat!
Mother, brother, father and me,
All of us together
In perfect harmony!
A hug here,
A hug there,
Love is in the air!

Taylor Cochrane (11)
Skegness Academy, Skegness

Baby Katie

Baby Katie is like a dog,
Zooming around the house all day,
Scavenging for food,
Dancing in the nude,
Screaming in every different way.

She gives a wink,
When her nappy stinks
And roars when she has it changed,
When she sees a socket
She shoots like a rocket
And fiddles with the mains.

Oh Baby Katie, how could you be gone?
Moved to Australia where the sun is strong,
Oh Baby Katie, I miss you, I do!
I thought we were stuck together by glue.

Leah Banwell (11)
Stafford Grammar School, Stafford

Smudge

There was a cat named Smudge,
He was scruffy and fluffy and as black as coal,
His tongue was as rough as sand and his paws as smooth as velvet.

He was lazy and dazy and always sleepy,
Crazy for fuss, a tickle or a hug,
Oh Smudge,
Oh Smudge,
You little black puss.

Thomas Stockton (12)
Stafford Grammar School, Stafford

The Girl With The Blue Eyes

She came to me and smiled
I did not know her name
She did not speak, she did not shout
But still I played her game

She beckoned me to follow
I fell under her spell
Her golden hair dazzled me
Though I did not know her well

I wondered what her name was
But I didn't dare to ask
Her flawless skin was ivory
Almost like a mask

Her hands were shaped so beautifully
They moved like butterflies
She moved them once, she moved them twice
But still I heard her cries

Her face was carved by angels
It was beautifully made
Her face began to glisten
And she began to fade

All that was left was a glint
As the sun set in the skies
The pale light above me
Was the girl with the blue eyes.

Amy Walker (13)
Stafford Grammar School, Stafford

The Elephant

The elephant wanted to be a monk,
He packed up his trunk
And set off on a junk,
The trouble was he was such a hunk
He sank the junk and lost his trunk.

He swam ashore and met a boar,
Who stated he was very poor,
The elephant said, 'What a bore to be so poor.'
When all he wanted was to be more
Than just a boar that is so poor.

Off they set to find a vet,
Whom in fact, they'd never met,
He said that he had a house to let,
But they weren't allowed to keep a pet,
They could however, live together and call each other Pet.

In the let without the vet,
They decided to set up a monastery,
They shaved their heads
And burnt their beds
The elephant was now so poor
And the boar that was still a bore.

Ben Colclough (13)
Stafford Grammar School, Stafford

The Wolf

The mountain is quiet, nothing dares move,
Then on comes the pitch-black wolf, being sleek and smooth
Down he comes, he's seen his prey,
Poor little rabbit, it's the end of her day.
With one running tackle, baring his teeth,
The rabbit to die atop of the heath.
They roll down the hill, like in a crazy dance,
The wolf looks ready to pounce.
The rabbit disappears in a frenzy of fur,
The wolf has won in a full on blur.
Everything goes quiet, the wolf creeps away,
Just before the birth of a brand new day.
Two or three hours after dawn,
The hunter wakes up with a long and loud yawn.
The horses come at amazing pace,
The wolf is losing the final race.
The hunter shoots, *bang!* A roar,
The wolf hits the hard, cold floor.
Nothing happens, the hunt goes away,
The wolf gets up, he chooses to die another day.

Joshua Hake (11)
Stafford Grammar School, Stafford

The Price Of War

Stepping off the jet
Onto hard, rocky ground
The searing heat that I let
Into my eyes is profound
I look to my left, seeing thousands of men
As I step into the lion's den.

Thousands of soldiers trudging with hope
A muddy pack slung on their back
As they struggle so hard to cope
Through the capital city of bomb hit Iraq
I'm disorientated, my head starts to spin
That's when the screams begin.

I throw myself on the ink-like mud
My sergeant shouting to get in formation
Looking at my leg, it's stained with blood
But we all move into location
I take on the job of leading the front line
The killing of the innocent, the only crime.

I take cover behind an empty shed
Helicopters whirring above me
Many of my comrades are already dead
Coming into war, that's the fee
Never for my country will I hide and cower
The fight for democracy, the battle for power.

After one whole hour, I see one with a broken wrist
As pale as milk, her arms shaking
No older than 6, she was caught in the midst
A bullet wound to her stomach, no acting, no faking
Picking her up in my arms, she was surprisingly light
The life draining out of her, she holds on to me with all her might.

I can feel Death's presence right beside me
The medics and doctors try everything
'Breathe,' they say to the girl, 'Take it easy,'
Many say that this is simple, which is far from the real thing
The little girl, before she dies tries to speak
'Mum,' she says as a tear falls down her cheek.

Ajay Mohan (13)
Stafford Grammar School, Stafford

Love

I don't need Sherlock,
I don't need Christie
I don't need Poirot
To solve this mystery.

Me and you
We have a connection,
In my eyes
You are perfection.

I feel your love,
You can sense mine,
How can I tell you?
You're damn fine.

I'll buy you jewellery,
I'll buy you clothes,
I'll buy you a car
If I can take you home.

I know what this is
And you do too,
How can I say this?
I love you.

Alex Urwin (13)
Stafford Grammar School, Stafford

The Fear

The boys were getting ready
Their voices shouting loud
The adrenaline was really pumping
As they marched to the sound

The guns were being loaded
The atmosphere was tense
The battlefield was waiting
Let the fight commence!

The boys they darted forwards
In and out the trees
Shots rang in the distance
Someone fell down to their knees

It felt like war was breaking
The fear it seemed real
All the boys had now been hit
A shout, a cry, a squeal

You might think someone was killed
A violent blow been struck
But only coloured paint was used
Thank goodness, what good luck!

Eliot Jeffries (13)
Stafford Grammar School, Stafford

I Forgot My Homework Miss

I forgot my homework, Miss
It's really not my fault
My dog came up and ate it
I did tell him to halt.

I forgot my homework, Miss
But it wasn't actually me
You should blame my monkey
Yes . . . he thought it was a flea!

I know it was my science, Miss
I'm really very sorry
I really didn't mean to
I was in a hurry.

I am so stupid, Miss
Now I mean it, true
I know I was so terrible
I forgot it was you

And now Miss, one more excuse
I feel I should mention
Oh no, don't tell me that
I got a detention.

Angus Inglis-Jones (12)
Stafford Grammar School, Stafford

Without You

Without you the sun won't shine,
Without you the birds won't sing,
Without you the stars won't glisten.

Without you there won't be happiness,
Without you there won't be love,
Without you there won't be warmth.

Without you I won't want to get out of bed,
Without you I won't want to brush my teeth,
Without you I won't want to have a shower.

Without you the cows won't moo,
Without you the bees won't buzz,
Without you the sheep won't baa.

Without you there won't be joy,
Without you there won't be laughter,
Without you there won't be smiles.

Without you I won't want to eat,
Without you I won't want to sleep,
Without you I won't want to live.

Without you . . .

Matthew Bond (13)
Stafford Grammar School, Stafford

Sheona, The Cat Burglar

(Dedicated to the sneaky one of my two corgis, Sheona)

My dog is a cat burglar,
She lives by the name of Sheona.
Oh, haven't you heard of her
Being as cunning as a snake?
But also, as silent as a mouse.
Waiting 'til all our backs are turned,
She seeks out her target,
Creeping across the silent room.

In the criminal's line up,
You know,
If the eyes are gazing or the head is tilted,
Which one did it?
Yes, Sheona's the one!

For I think the term should be changed
To dog burglar.
For many have shed tears
For their great loss of slippers and teddy.

For we all know the culprit . . .
Oh Sheona, come over here.

Jamie Baker (11)
Stafford Grammar School, Stafford

Don't Let Them Pass Your Lips

What is love?
What is sorrow?
Don't let them pass your lips.
So brave and strong, yet still so young
Can't quite see what's amiss.

Take what you need
And walk away
To claim your promised ending
But truly, what was there to take?
Nothing worth defending.

What is love?
What is sorrow?
Don't let them pass your lips.
Though old and spent, I've no regrets
At least, dear child know this:

Words like love
Words like sorrow
They really don't exist
Remember who I am, girl, so
Don't let them pass your lips.

Ann Lu (14)
Stafford Grammar School, Stafford

Holbrook Grange Bouquet

One winter afternoon,
The type that is crisp and clear,
Mum and her friend took me
To see a little pony.

I thought it was for my mum's friend's niece,
But they were fooling me,
For on the 25th December
There stood the little pony,
The best pony ever
And always will be.

A white blaze runs down her face,
It looks like a lightning bolt,
But when she gallops she goes at a very fast pace.
I will always love her.

Lucy Allen (11)
Stafford Grammar School, Stafford

What Time Is It?

Wrapper ripping,
Brandy tipping,
Ribbon tying,
Flower drying.

Picture painting,
Money hating,
Tree choosing,
Morning snoozing.

Turkey munching,
Snow crunching,
Stocking piggle,
Children giggle.

But what time is it?

Amber Towers (12)
Stafford Grammar School, Stafford

162

The Lonely Soldier

The damp, dark trench
Black rats scurry about as if not wanting to be seen.
The brief clatter of machine gun fire
Allied men falling everywhere.
While a lonely soldier shivers in the trench
A solitary puff on his pipe
Waiting to go over.

The distant battle approaching steadily
The regiment awakes from its sleep
The grinding of metal from the bayonets
The shouting of orders from the sergeant.
Silence, the soldiers standing to attention
A single whistle blow

It's time to go over the top.

Cameron Kendall (12)
Stafford Grammar School, Stafford

The Cat

Jeremy, the tabby, was a moggy
And his brain was astonishingly foggy
He liked beans and his pet doggy
But loathed parsnips and getting soggy.

One day, Jeremy sat in a bowl of peas
He ate some smelly gorgonzola cheese
The cheese gave him wobbly knees
And he staggered over to some wonky trees.

Under the trees, Jeremy discovered a jolly rat
Wearing its best suit and an orange top hat
'You look unconventional,' said the cat
'Did you dress in the dark? You're not a bat!'

Holly Packham (12)
Stafford Grammar School, Stafford

Stupid Bullying

I try to work
Although you distract me
With constant mithering
And stupid bullying.

I give my best in life
But nothing's easy
All due to you
And your stupid bullying.

I get all As
Due to my hard work
But you don't like it
And decide to use that
Stupid bullying!

Jeremy Housden (13)
Stafford Grammar School, Stafford

Thou Knighted

Thou knighted, thou knighted, as you were great,
Thou knighted, thou knighted, there was no complaint.
Thou knighted, thou knighted, your powers were strong,
Thou knighted, thou knighted, you had many a song.
Thou knighted, thou knighted, you were a United,
Thou knighted, thou knighted, and 7s were sighted.
Thou knighted, thou knighted, your tactics were fantastic,
Thou knighted, thou knighted, you made other teams look drastic!
Thou knighted, thou knighted, a plane crash you survived,
Thou knighted, thou knighted, your soul forever will survive.

Oh, the best manager you're sure to be,
So we'll follow the name Sir Matthew Busby.

Gemma Brough (11)
Stafford Grammar School, Stafford

The Tree

The tree was as green as the sky,
It was like a doorknob,
It was as tall as a piece of string
And had branches as fat as lumps of cheese.

The tree was also as clever as a football,
It acted like a chair,
It was like a curtain
And as deaf as a chicken.

When it was young the tree was as tiny as a computer,
It was like a felt tip pen,
It was as noisy as a dictionary
And as smelly as a box.

Chloe Banner (11)
Stafford Grammar School, Stafford

Moods

Illness
Confused
Hurt
Violent
Angry
Funny
Enjoyed
Excited
Worried
Daydreaming
Difficult
Talkative
Abusive
Mardy.

Scott McIvor (16)
The Fountains High School, Burton-on-Trent

My Moods

I sometimes get angry but it's okay
I keep it bottled up inside
Till it blows up in my face

I sometimes get upset but it's okay
I'll just cheer myself up playing my guitar

I sometimes get confused but it's okay
I'll just go ask Mum about what's confused me

I sometimes get annoyed but it's okay
I just go somewhere
Quiet like my room
Because nobody's allowed in

Sometimes I am silly but it's okay
Because I like being silly sometimes
It makes people laugh

Sometimes I'm good but it's okay
Because I like being good sometimes
Because I don't like being told off

I sometimes get fed up but it's okay
Because I'll keep going till I've done it

Sometimes I'm hyper but it's okay
Mum just tells me to calm down a bit

I sometimes feel scared but it's okay
I just go give Mum a hug and talk to Mum about it

Sometimes I feel violent but it's okay
I'll just play on my Xbox and shoot some people

All these moods are okay because they are my moods.

Ryan Seville (15)
The Fountains High School, Burton-on-Trent

Miracles Do Happen

A lifetime of darkness is what they feared,
Not seeing the ones they held dear.
In the depths of despair they had no hope, only prayers,
Something from nothing was what they thought they could hear.

Seventeen days passed without hope,
But all throughout they seemed to cope.
Then a breath of luck blew on the thirty,
Could this be the end of their upset and pain?

Workers piled in, trying to drill the hole,
To give resources to the men so bold.
The workers sent food and devices,
All the belief going to their saviours.

Another hole was being drilled,
A hole that never can be filled.
After sixty-six days the miners appear,
The assembled crowd gave a rapturous cheer.

A twenty minute journey from the bottom to the top,
A twenty minute journey from the darkness to the light.

Reunited with their families is what matters now,
Exhausted but happy,
Smiling faces, eyes glistening and a new future was assured.

Khalil McGuinness (12)
The Lancaster School, Leicester

Valentines

Every February 14th
I'll go out and get my best suit pressed,
Ironed, cleaned.
Squeezed between the heat of industry.

I'll walk from the dry cleaners to the barber shop,
I'll get a haircut,
Snip to my fringe and sides,
Letting my hair drop to the
Cold, tiled floor,
Like DNA meteors.

I'll walk from the barber shop to the liquor shop,
I'll pick the finest wine available,
Red, like heavy hearts,
Sparkling like diamonds,
Shimmering like dew on the summer grass.

I'll walk from the liquor shop to the music shop,
I'll buy a record filled with the songs we adore,
Love through crochets and quavers,
Background noise to the conversations of happiness
Just spinning slowly under the needle.

I'll walk from the music shop to the book shop
I'll buy a book filled with recipes for couples,
Dishes to tempt a palate as divine as yours,
Prepared thoroughly with love
And served to you with passion.

I'll walk from the book shop to our place,
I'll put on my pressed, clean suit
And do my snipped, trimmed hair
And pour out the red, sparkling wine
And put on the loving, slow record
And make the divine, passionate food
And then I'll sit
And I'll wait
And I'll pretend you're coming home tonight.

Aaron Byrne (15)
The Prior Academy LSST, Lincoln

The Mystery Man In The Black Coat

That's him again, on the street
He sits there every night
I wonder who he is sometimes
The mystery man in the black coat.

He has a big bag with him
I want to know what's in it
Maybe it is something magical
A mystery never heard of.

He looked up at me the other night
I had never seen his face before
His big blue eyes stared into mine
Like a feeling I'd never felt before.

I wanted to go and see him
To find out who he was
And tell me why he sat there at night
In that big, black coat.

I waited for him again that night
I stared outside my window
Waiting for him to come and look at me again
Will he reveal his mystery?

He didn't look up at me tonight
I'm not sure that he ever will
The mystery's not unravelling
Like I thought it would do.

I always stare at him sitting in the street
Trying to work out answers
For the questions I wish to ask
I wonder who he is
The mystery man in the black coat.

Olivia Crowther (12)
The Prior Academy LSST, Lincoln

Waiting There For Me

I long to go back home again,
Away from sand and sea,
I want to see my friends again
And it not just be me.

I long to walk into my room
And see my precious treasures,
I want to smell the scent of home
And feel the familiar pleasures.

I long to call my cousin
And hear her cheery sound,
I want to tell her where I've been
And invite her to come around.

I long to see my cat again
And give him lots of fuss,
I want to stroke his silken fur
And cuddle my charming puss.

I long to eat my Sunday dinner
With roast beef and Yorkshire pud,
I want to taste that treacle sponge,
The aroma that smells so good.

I long to have a leisurely soak,
With the bubbles all hot and steamy,
I want to stay in there for hours
And feel relaxed and dreamy.

I long to go back home again,
Away from sand and sea,
I want to be back in my own bed
And have Teddy waiting there for me.

Bethany Williams
The Prior Academy LSST, Lincoln

We're Doing All We Can

Gust of wind caresses my cheek
Doubt I'll be able to sleep for a week;
Familiar smells, sharp and stinging
The personnel bustle, a phone is ringing.
A nurse strolls past, her smile all too brief
Performing her duties to bring relief;
To the tortured souls, lives tainted with ill
Some keep going, some lose the will.

A bed rattles through, the man is serene
Though maybe the drugs are making him dream
For who would relax in such a place,
Who'd have such a broad grin on their face?
Wires thread through his prominent veins
Like shiny snakes, like bounding chains;
Writhing round the ice-white skin
Alongside hurries his next of kin.
The golden ring stands proudly on her thin finger
Fear mingled with her smile, I cannot linger;
But I must, though I admit I hate with a passion
A place where pain is simply the fashion.

A little old lady is hunched in the corner
The reality is here, it has dawned upon her;
Her slight spine curves, she hunches and rocks
Tears fall under her soft, grey locks.

I eye the clock, the hands slip slow
As the only ones that are in the know
Come bustling out of the sterile doors
Looking for family, no relation of yours . . .

Victoria Taylor (15)
The Prior Academy LSST, Lincoln

Freedom

All I want is freedom
To be not bossed around
All I want is freedom
To hear a happy sound

All I want is freedom
To have something to eat
All I want is freedom
To have something on my feet

All I want is freedom
To have something to drink
All I want is freedom
To have some time to think

All I want is freedom
No shouting in my ear
All I want is freedom
For my family to be here

To be nice and warm
All I want is freedom
Why was I born?

All I want is freedom
To be not bossed around
All I want is freedom
To hear a happy sound.

Imogen Vivian
The Prior Academy LSST, Lincoln

Britain

Britain is an island
Isolated, protected and preserved.

Britain is a jungle,
Of concrete, steel and wood.

Britain is a survivor,
Persevering, pushing and hunting.

Britain is a leader,
Persuading, teaching and motivating.

Britain is a fighter,
Charging, firing and pursuing.

Britain is lost,
Searching, roaming and finding.

Britain is a pioneer,
Mapping, creating and inventing.

Britain is fading,
Threatened, unrecognised and suppressed.

Gregory Harrison (13)
The Prior Academy LSST, Lincoln

The Daydreamer

The sky is beautiful
The swirls are silver
The sky is black with silver stars
It's so hassle free
I wish I was a star, shining bright
With not a care in the world
I can see it now
I'm shining the brightest
If only I was living on my own
It would be a hassle-free life.

Anna Dawson (11)
The Prior Academy LSST, Lincoln

Down A Hole

Blind,
Folded into the echoing burrow.

And there I patiently abided,
Whilst every moment whipped to and fro,
Vigorously, yet alone.

The unseen, the forbidden -
Perhaps better known,
As soft agony, brutal and bleak,
Where I search,
Where I seek,
Where I desire,
My master's key.

Hereafter, unleashed from Hell's fire,
I long to see,
I long to sense,
I long to feel,
Nature's true beauty.

Tasnim Hassan (15)
The Prior Academy LSST, Lincoln

Happy Birthday!

Happy birthday, happy birthday! I just wanted to say
Happy birthday, happy birthday! Your birthday's in May.
Happy birthday, happy birthday! I got you a gift
Happy birthday, happy birthday! I hope it gives you a lift?
Happy birthday, happy birthday! You're a day older than before
Happy birthday, happy birthday! You're too old for the seesaw
Happy birthday, happy birthday! Blow out the flame
Happy birthday, happy birthday! Tomorrow you won't be the same
Happy birthday, happy birthday! Then let's all say
Hip, hip . . . hooray!

Simone Summan Nath (11)
The Prior Academy LSST, Lincoln

The Family Home

Into the base add three teaspoons of love,
Mix in one teaspoon of fairness and respect,
To bring the family together add in a briefcase of excitement
And adrenaline,
Add to the mixture half a teaspoon of rivalry.

Into the walls add one TV with a Sky box,
Hammer in the family movies to give enjoyment,
Paint the walls with the fun of the family
And with happiness as there is no tomorrow.

Into the ceiling add the Christmas tree and Easter toys,
Mix it with other family fun and frivolity,
Paint it with the memories of times gone by,
Hammer in the family portraits.

Into the roof mix the sense of safety,
Add to that the comfort of the home,
Mix until the home is ready
And then let the family roam.

Euan Kelly (12)
The Prior Academy LSST, Lincoln

The Volcano Of Death

The smell of sulphur smashed through the village
And birds fell from trees like rain,
Screaming children sounded like knives
To anybody listening.

Everybody was choking on ash
And many people lay dead, a large hole in their chests,
Made by the boiling tears of the monstrosity
That lay waste to the village.

The lava streaming down its slopes was as hot as the sun
And as destructive as a hurricane,
The volcano was an angry superior, punishing the village for its sins
And if you looked at all the people running,
It was as if the village had grown legs and run away.
The villagers ran, but to no avail,
The eruption was faster than any man.

Then silence, no life, no sound,
Just ash and rock.

Callum Janssen (11)
The Prior Academy LSST, Lincoln

The Bonfire

As warm as the sun
The bonfire's embers crackle intensely,
So intense that just the embers could light a forest fire,
The wood snaps and burns like glass smashing under the pressure.
The warmth of the bonfire heats the people around it,
Making people feel grateful for the wood used to make it.
But nothing can last forever,
It has to stop burning eventually,
The bonfire slowly starts to fade,
The bonfire slowly faded as the wood burnt to ash.

Joshua Hewitt (11)
The Prior Academy LSST, Lincoln

My Dream House

My dream house will be on the tropical borders of Barbados,
Calm trees shall be the corners of this exotic sanctuary.
Bamboo canes filled with respect and grown with care
Are my walls.
Golden sand sprinkled with love.
A giant bed, soaked with prosperity by the everlasting sunshine.
At night, stars look down upon me with an ancient eye while I lay,
Stationary, with a sleepy head
Crystal teardrops from my eye filled with joy
Ready for another amazing day.

Alexander Hogg (12)
The Prior Academy LSST, Lincoln

My Seven Dogs

One dog, two dog, three dog, four,
There are so many, please no more,
Five dog, six dog, seven dogs too,
Wait, did I miscount, let me go through,
Savannah like grasslands,
Tia who commands land,
Summer, just so bright,
Kali, annoying like flea bites,
Mia, the little baby,
Jabari is nothing but lazy,
He is also brave yet wimpy,
Akili, phew! So stinky,
They slobber and beg,
They all walk on four legs,
Dog prints here and there,
I say this because I care,
They cause nothing but mayhem,
Although I must say I will always love them!

Georgina Hanson-Davalos (14)
The Prior Academy LSST, Lincoln

My Perfect World

Would have . . .
My friends and family surrounding me.
No world of hatred or war, just peace.
The world of no hunger or greed.

A world of love filled to the brim,
The place would have no jealousy or bullies
Or anything that would be horrible.

Because my world isn't just about me and what I want,
It's about you and the needy.

Daniel Mead (12)
The Prior Academy LSST, Lincoln

House Of Death

Death creeps through the hallways,
Blood drips on the floor,
Previous owners' bodies
Are stapled to the doors.

The highway to Hell ends here,
The rain never stops,
A storm is always brewing
Even if it's not.

Why did God create this?
It's a shortcut to Hell,
They'll remember this place in time,
At the tolling of the bells.

The Greeks, they had a name for it,
They called it 'Pandora's Box'
It used to be a fairy tale
But now it's been unlocked.

Dominic Scoines (11)
The Prior Academy LSST, Lincoln

My Dream World

Build my walls with pictures of my friends,
Fill the floor with flowers, like there's no end,
Stick my family tree in a bright, sporty scrapbook,
Fasten on all of my snow-white hooks.

Colour the ceiling with muddy footprints,
On top of each pillow there must be a mint,
Carry in all of my clothes,
Make sure the grass is neatly mowed.

Screw together the sound of waves crashing,
The soothing scent of potatoes mashing,
Glue in place all of my thoughts,
Fill up my sweetie jar with all sorts.

Make my roof out of candy canes,
Turn the rain into sugar grains,
Transform my unicorn from black to red,
Make my future look great ahead.

Charlotte Ramscar (12)
The Prior Academy LSST, Lincoln

Bonfire Night

The fire sparkled like the sun
The fireworks jumped into the air using trampolines
The noise was as loud as a volcano erupting
Nothing could drown the noise out
The smell of burning was blowing into my face
You could see the embers flying off the fire
You could barely open your eyes
As the fire shone so bright
Everyone was walking around with pretty sparklers
You need to wrap up warm
Even though the fire is as hot as anything
Bonfire Night is beautiful.

Amelia Gratton (11)
The Prior Academy LSST, Lincoln

Good Times

My life is full of family, friends and fun,
Sledging in the snow and picnics in the sun.
Things to remember without any reasons,
Good times turning up throughout all seasons.

Friends for little school playing in the park,
Racing, chasing, being home before dark.
Friends at big school, happily forever,
Joining clubs, sharing lunch, working to get clever.

Holidays at Disneyland, special days out,
Theme parks, zoos and beaches, generally messing about.
Memories and photographs of all these happy days,
Camcorders coming out for assemblies and Christmas plays.

A floppy rag doll, Noo-Noo, named when I was two,
A family who love me and everything I do.
A hug and a smile, hot chocolate in my best cup,
That's what's good when you're growing up!

Lauryn Fleming
The Prior Academy LSST, Lincoln

Homely

Walls of chocolate
Bed of steel
Nothing's more homely than
My favourite meal

A floor of friendship
A roof of balloons
Nothing's more homely than
A view of the moon

A forest as a garden
A waterfall in the pond
Nothing's more homely than
A good family bond!

Adam Welchman [12]
The Prior Academy LSST, Lincoln

Tiny

At my height everything seems
Always too far out of reach for me.
There is a place I can go
Where I grow tall and nobody knows.
When I am tall I can see
Everything down below me.
Then I realise, I can't reach the key.

I have just stopped going to that place
And have just come back from outer space.
Being small is no gift you know,
It's something to be proud of,
Not a freak show!

Katherine Gilman-Abel [11]
The Prior Academy LSST, Lincoln

A World A Long Way Away

I'd hammer the hate
Polish the happiness
Screw together the love and respect
Raise the sense of our races' pride
Fasten the hopes of a lost cause
That one day evil will ride away
Leaving us foundations
Of a world a long way away.

Jeremy Stewart (12)
The Prior Academy LSST, Lincoln

The Weather Poem

I can hear the rain, can you hear the rain?
Pitta-patta! Pitta-patta! I can hear the rain.

It's stopped . . .
Here it comes again, the heavy, stormy rain.
Pitta-flash! Patta-crash! I hate the stormy rain.

I can see the snow, can you see the snow?
Freeze-fall, freeze-fall! I can see the snow.

It's stopped . . .
I'm playing in the snow, the light, white snow.
Freeze-stomp! Fall-romp! I like the white snow.

I can feel the sun, can you feel the sun?
Heat-shine! Heat-shine! I can feel the sun.

It's stopped . . .
It's coming back for fun, the warm rosy sun.
Heat-sun! Heat-sun! I love rosy sun.

Abigail Churchill (11)
The Prior Academy LSST, Lincoln

Flying High

In the midnight sky
Twinkling stars are flying high,
Like diamonds
Up above me,
Hidden treasures for all the world to see.

Glistening beautifully,
In the crisp, cold air,
The moon, as pure as snow,
Brings colour to this stage,
Giving the performance of a lifetime.

As I look up high into the deep unknown,
The sky cascades around me,
Draping vibrant colours about my shoulders,
The crash of cymbals as they join
And loop the loop as they swirl and dance
Above my head.

Natalie-Jade Botterill (11)
The Prior Academy LSST, Lincoln

What Matters To Me

Everyone has something that matters to them
It may be a book, a pet or a sparkly gem
But the thing that matters the most to me
Is my godmother and her name is Ellie.

She's kooky and funny and one of a kind
She's wild and crazy and out of her mind
Her house is in Wales near the River Wye
It's often cold but it's worth a try.

Ellie has two dogs and a three-legged cat
Ducks and chickens roam the yard
But trying to catch them is really quite hard.

Ellie makes me feel so happy
Her sense of humour is sharp and snappy
She's kind and loving and gives me plenty to do
She's my mum's best friend, but she loves me too.

Elliot Hollamby
The Prior Academy LSST, Lincoln

Things That Matter

Hammer the ice cream into the foundations
Screw the chocolate together to make the floorboards
Stick in the lovely fridge
And fill it with delicious food.

Build glorious walls of music
Hammer a TV into each room
Like a house of technology
Bring in the respect and nail it to the floor.

Paint the calmness into each door
The house is a sanctuary of peace
Bring in the kindness and nail it to the roof
Fill the garden with golden sand.

The garden a beach, none the less
Fences made from sunbeds and food stands
Happiness all around.

Matthew Gray (12)
The Prior Academy LSST, Lincoln

The Haunted House

The door cried for oil as it was opened,
The house shook violently; it threw people all over.
The candyfloss cobwebs draped the house,
The staircase looked like a bulldozer had run over it.
The dust downstairs reached a foot,
The mirror looked like it had shattered
And been roughly placed back together.
The mice scuttled along the skirting board,
The wind whistled a sad tune repeatedly.
The boarded up windows gave a claustrophobic feeling.
The girl jumped back three metres
When she saw the arachnid academy.
An oppressive feeling of doom and gloom hung over the house,
A ghost's eyes reflected in the mirror,
Everyone ran for their lives . . .

Edward Borchardt (11)
The Prior Academy LSST, Lincoln

Sunset

The sun is a million fireflies
Glowing and turning up high,
Colours leaping
Through the evening.

Oranges, yellows, reds and greens,
All so beautiful, like a dream.
The sun was so bright,
Now fading to night.

Sunlight so pale
That ends the day's tale.
For now it's in bed
To rest its weary head.

God bless you Sun!

Saskia Dowley (11)
The Prior Academy LSST, Lincoln

Childhood

Can you remember when you were a child?
Everything seemed like it smiled
The teddy bears that have been and gone
But the summer sun still shone
How many houses have you had?
And the cleaning that made your mum mad
Is there a farm near you or even a park?
I'm twelve and I haven't seen a shark
There are many things that go into a home
Love and hate and a garden gnome
Quick everyone, inside, there is a storm brewing
Can you hear the cows mooing?
The chimney smoke goes up high
I hope I stay here till I die.

Oliver Higginson (12)
The Prior Academy LSST, Lincoln

Bonfire Night

Everyone is muffled in heaps of clothes
Outside in the bitter cold,
The fire in front of me sizzles and pops away,
Making familiar noises.
The colours of orange and yellow dazzle my eyes,
It starts to die out and turns into just grey smoke.

I feel disappointed,
Then suddenly, *bang!* Everyone jumps with surprise,
It's the fireworks, ready to play!
Then a beautiful splash of colour pops into the sky,
Making different patterns in the foggy atmosphere
And sprinkles again into the sky,
Like a toddler with a paintbrush splashing it on the page.

Sasha Hate (11)
The Prior Academy LSST, Lincoln

Sadlers Wells 2009

London lights
Shining bright
Crowds of thousands
On a Sunday night

Hours and hours
Of rehearsing routines
Costumes and fundraising
Setting the scene

Show day is here
Inside I feel fear
Nerves and excitement
As the performance draws near

Show has started
Ready to dance
I feel so happy
To be offered the chance

As I step on stage
The nerves have all gone
What a magical feeling
As we finally shone

At the side of the stage
Teachers are beaming
As the audience applauds
Our last dance of the evening

Families surround us
Faces full of delight
What a fabulous memory
Of a wonderful night.

Bethany McMellon (11)
Thomas Telford School, Telford

My Own Way

He barks to come in,
He barks to go out,
So in unison we all do shout,
'Let the dog in, let the dog out.'
But in his mind he has no doubt . . .
They will get up!

He has two meals a day, a real meaty treat,
But every night as we're sitting to eat,
There he is, right by our side,
His tail wagging and big eyes open wide,
He's told off for begging every night,
But he takes no notice, he just thinks we're tight,
They will feed me!

Then bath, teas bed we all do go,
He has other ideas, he's in the know,
If I jump high enough I can just make the bed,
Move off that pillow, I need room for my head,
'Bertie, keep still!' no matter how loud we shout,
There's no way he's moving or getting out,
They will let me sleep here!

Our four-legged friend knows the score,
He's a spoilt, pampered pooch, with requests galore,
He's part of our family and loved like a brother,
There's no way he would be swapped for another,
They will let me have my own way!

Harvey Worrall (11)
Thomas Telford School, Telford

Sixty Degrees - Haiku

Sweat rolls off hot flesh
Sixty degree heatwave caught
Bodies unaware.

Luca Zammuto (12)
Thomas Telford School, Telford

My Teacher Is A Bee!

It happened at the end of the day,
Just as we were going out to play,
She was standing near the sink,
Then she began to shrink!

Her clothes were falling all around,
She was making an awful sound,
As her clothes came popping off,
She looked like a fuzzy cloth.

As her clothes dropped round her knees,
Her skin started looking like a bee's!
What made her change? What made her pop?
Was it the time of our clock?

Antennae were sprouting on her head,
As she pelted us with pencil lead,
Then we heard an awful ring,
She was letting out her sting!

As she flew at us in a rage,
A very stupid girl called Page,
Got in her (teacher's) way and woe betide,
Her teacher stung her with her behind!

We all ran outside,
'Our teacher's using her behind!
She's gone mad I tell you,
She should be put in London Zoo!'

Holly Martin (11)
Thomas Telford School, Telford

Earthquakes

Streets shake
Ground rumbles
Huge buildings
Quickly crumble

Roads crack
Bridges part
Nothing the same
As at the start

Dust flies
Rubble is still
Dirt slides
Holes are filled

Hundreds gone
Thousands missing
People searching
Hoping
Wishing

No shelter
Damage done
This battle is lost
The Earth has won.

Aimee Chambers (12)
Thomas Telford School, Telford

Fire

Fire, warm as the sun,
Sparkling light,
Glowing bright,
A warming sensation when you come in from the snow,
An exciting heat as it melts your marshmallow,
Flames of yellow, orange and red,
Relaxing you before you go to bed.

Kelly Wong (11)
Thomas Telford School, Telford

Granny Di

With bleached blonde hair
And ceramic teeth
Hugs galore
And trifle deep
My granny.

With fluffy jumpers
And fleecy slippers
Sweets a'plenty and
Blackpool trippers
My granny.

A rabbit called Cheesy
And a big, ugly scar
A hatred of green
A mobility car
My granny

She got confused
And fell asleep
Wires and machines
All go beep - then quiet
My granny.
I miss you.

Kiaya Plimmer (12)
Thomas Telford School, Telford

192

The Land Of Sweets

There once was a land of sweets
And many more tasty treats
There were liquorice roads
And jelly toads!

To get there were chocolate stairs
And at the top I was greeted by gummy bears
There were then lots of gingerbread men
And a chocolate Big Ben!

The trees were lollipops
And there were lots of sweet shops
But you didn't need to buy any
Because you got them for less than a penny!

There were candy canes
And chocolate planes
And candyfloss flowers
And flake twin towers!

The whole world was made out of sweets
And everyone enjoyed these treats
I had loads of fun
Until I was woken by my mum.

Isobel Manley (11)
Thomas Telford School, Telford

Barney

Barney is my big, black dog,
He sleeps all day, dreaming of bones,
His coat is shiny and bright,
He looks at me lovingly with his cute puppy dog eyes,
He wags his tail from side to side,
He loves his food and walks,
He is my pet, my pet, Barney.

Alex Wood (11)
Thomas Telford School, Telford

The Robot

You can use an iPod to listen to music
You can use a computer to research anything
You can use a mobile to contact friends
You can use a TV to watch movies
You can use a radio to explore music
You can use a DS to play games all over the world.

Tom Postane (11)
Thomas Telford School, Telford

My Wicked Stepmother

My wicked, wicked stepmother . . .
The very, very worst -
It's as if the witches of the west had her cursed.
She makes me clean up and do all the chores
And I have to do them all or she lets a humungous
Roars!

My wicked, wicked stepmother . . .
The very, very worst -
She never hands me a penny, she keeps it all in a purse
And what makes the matter even worse,
Is that she keep it in a safe -
Now how am I meant to know that combination of hers!

She never feeds me a decent chicken meal
Instead at meal times she will reveal
A bowl of soup and water which isn't much of a bother -
Then the next day in the toilet I may have to hover!

My wicked, wicked stepmother . . .
The very, very best, I'd never, ever swap her,
Not even for a gold threaded vest!

Athen Newdell (11)
Thomas Telford School, Telford

The Old Oak Tree

The old oak tree, the old oak tree,
What can you say about the old oak tree?
It's ancient and wise,
But there's a surprise,
As when you see it,
You will believe it,
As you see the bark, eroded by age,
It's like looking at a crowded page,
When you see is at night,
It's like looking at shepherd's delight.
The hard, rough and soft textures of the tree,
Like a collision of Audi TT's.
The twigs are frail, like an old lady,
However, in the summer the leaves grow back and it's all shady.
Whooshes and woos are the leaves pirouetting in the wind.
Winter's day arrives and the old dustbin man from across the road
Comes and rakes them all up, ready to be binned.
The old oak tree has lots of memories and times,
But every day's a struggle as two worlds collide,
The old oak tree, the old oak tree,
Wouldn't you like to see the old oak tree?

Millie Grundy (12)
Thomas Telford School, Telford

Friendship

Friendship gets you through thick and thin,
When you're in a battle you'll always win.
Friends love, care and protect you,
They always help and respect you.
When everyone else leaves you all alone,
Your true friends come and bring you home.
They stand beside you and never forget you,
They will listen with all their heart
And do their best to support you!

Lucy Connelly (11)
Thomas Telford School, Telford

The Tidal Wave

It's a monster in waiting,
But hides its natural beauty,
It sways like a fish, weaving in and out.

It sprays a mist to give a warning,
It breaks out of its cage.

It rocks a boat to take revenge,
It engulfs the Earth for its tea.

But the Earth survives this unpleasant scene . . .

Katie Kinnon (12)
Thomas Telford School, Telford

Tutankhamun's Curse

Tutankhamun's curse
There are hieroglyphics
On the walls, watching you.

Don't enter or else
Whoever enters will die
He is watching you.

Believe it or not
It will come true and kill you
Howard Carter entered.

He discovered all
Gold, silver and many treasures
Howard Carter . . . cursed.

Then some weeks later
Mysteriously dead
The curse had struck him.

How did this happen?
A coincidence or not?
Who will ever know?

Abigail Horton (13)
Thomas Telford School, Telford

Tsunami

As I looked out of my house that day
I thought I was at sea,
All the houses fishing boats,
The fish were you and me.

The streets were rippling rivers,
The fields I could not see,
The trees now seaweed in the water,
The fish were you and me.

Bang! Crash! A window smashed,
Sharp glass crushed my knee,
People panicked, parents paused,
The water too strong for me.

The stars were then the Devil's eyes,
Watching the fishes and me,
The sea was then his hands as well.
Crash!

Silence

The water too strong for me.

Laura Ali (12)
Thomas Telford School, Telford

My Brother Jack
(Age four, why not more?)

He's spilt his drink
He's dropped my iPod in the sink
He's left his tea
He's even thrown his cars at me
He's mean, he's cruel, he acts like a fool
He follows me, I look so un-cool
My brother Jack is such a pain
I wish we'd left him back in Spain!

But then again, there are those eyes
And those waves when he says goodbyes
His huge, cheesy grin
His sticky chocolate chin
His laughs and giggles when we enjoy a tickle
His funny made up words, like 'lello' and 'ickle'
My brother Jack can drive me insane
But I love him to bits and I shouldn't complain!

Charlotte Lucas (11)
Thomas Telford School, Telford

When I Went To Cosford

At Cosford I learnt about British medals and German too,
Our aircraft had an emblem of red, white and blue,
The German planes had two types of cross,
It was a shame that so much life was lost.

The Spitfires and Hurricanes fought in the skies,
The enemy were the Me109s,
Although things looked bad for us all,
The Battle of Britain was won,
Phew! That was a close call.

Matthew Newbold (11)
Thomas Telford School, Telford

That's Life

You start off as a baby going, 'Goo, goo, goo, goo, gaa'
Then, soon enough you're toddling round and round, hurrah
After that you're running like a lunatic
And before you know it drinking and being sick
After adolescence came knocking on your door
You find that's when life begins to become a chore
There's jobs to do and bills to pay, it never seems to end
And if you are a parent, you're sent right round the bend

Before you know it, retirement's here, with pensions on your mind
Life begins to slow a bit, allowing you to unwind
Sitting there doing crosswords, in your rocking chair
And looking in a mirror at your grey hair
Also in the mirror you can see the life you've had
Many happy memories, but why do you feel so sad?
Soon enough you're in hospital with masks and wires everywhere
But when you try to wake up, you're not even there!

Megan Boland Clark (11)
Thomas Telford School, Telford

Little Sisters

Little sisters are small but very funny,
They like to eat fish fingers to fill up their tummy,
Little, mucky handprints plastered on the wall,
Trying to stand on anything to make them ten feet tall.

Little monkeys jumping all around,
Up the staircase in pyjamas bound,
Little ones, time for your beds,
Time to rest those sleepy heads!

Mollie Morton-Hurcombe (11)
Thomas Telford School, Telford

Drought

Corpses surround the drought-hit waterhole
Meat more than two months old,
The grass not fed for what seemed to be more than a year,
A single spark and the Australian bush killer was upon the country.
Even the more advanced beings struggling,
The heat was as bad as if the sun had just moved in next door,
Had invited you in for a few minutes, with his cake in the oven.
The air reflected the sea,
Or what was left of it,
The white faces smiled at me, as if everything was okay.
Orange became everyone's least favourite colour,
We longed for the damp drops from the grey-blue sky,
The wet air,
The remaining organisms fled, fled to the coast,
Racoons were chatting to koalas, birds to kangaroos,
Longing for the drops, before they dropped.

Matthew Price (13)
Thomas Telford School, Telford

The Avalanche

The snow was crackling like a ticking time bomb,
Tick, tick! But when was it about to explode?
Five frozen fingers that couldn't move,
Four trees in the distance, swaying furiously,
Three layers of jumpers hanging on for dear life,
Two raging eyeballs about to pop out,
One lonely figure, nobody could hear or see,
Zero! A rush of thick slush pouring down the mountain
And that was that for me.

Sam Topper (12)
Thomas Telford School, Telford

Whether The Weather

Whether the weather is snowy,
It would be bitter cold and the freezing winds
would be nipping at your nose!
The snow would softly fall on the ground,
forming a crystal white blanket
And the sky would be blue, blue like the ocean,
But not as harsh, it would be still, calm, not a clumpy cloud in sight.

Whether the weather is sunny,
Who knows? The birds would be tweeting their little hearts out,
The sun would be blazing,
brightening up every little dark corner there is
And then there would be that one person who's day isn't so bright
And the sun would come gleaming, making their day a delight!

Whether the weather, who cares?
Somehow you will still have a great day!

Emmie Louca
Thomas Telford School, Telford

202

A Stormy Night

Darkening shadows hover above me,
Like an eagle searching for its prey.
That lonely, peeping star in the sky,
Fear like a chicken hiding from a fox.
Howling winds sends trees twisting and turning,
As they struggle to gather their stance.
I watch heavy raindrops plummet from the heavens
And smack against my windowsill.
Laughter of the thunder strikes again
And the poor animals outside take cover.
My heart sinks further and further into my cosy bed,
Whilst I watch and wait for one last strike.
Bang! A fork of lightning breaks through the sky,
Now it most certainly is a stormy night.

Lydia Kendrick (12)
Thomas Telford School, Telford

I Am

I am sport,
I am a brand new toy and the oldest castle,
I am tough, I am strong but I am fragile,
I am books,
I am TV,
I am sun,
I am moon,
I am light,
I am dark,
I am pen,
I am pencil,
I am dead and alive,
I am time,
I am song
And I am a window, I see right through you.

Conor Embrey (11)
Thomas Telford School, Telford

A Poem To Attract Your Family's Attention

(Inspired by 'Poem To Attract Mum's Attention' by Roger Stevens)

Tip: Try saying the poem with a variety of voices.

Dad
Dad
Dad
Bro
Bro
Bro
Sis
Sis
Sis
Mum
Mum
Mum.

Kay Wong (11)
Thomas Telford School, Telford

Young Writers Information

We hope you have enjoyed reading this
book - and that you will continue to enjoy it
in the coming years.

If you like reading and writing poetry drop
us a line, or give us a call, and we'll send
you a free information pack.

Alternatively if you would like to order further
copies of this book or any of our other titles,
then please give us a call or log onto our
website at www.youngwriters.co.uk

Young Writers Information
Remus House
Coltsfoot Drive
Peterborough
PE2 9BF
(01733) 890066